- Julia -
May you be blessed
in all you do and
always strive to
be your best you!
Nancy

CAREER COMPASS
for Women

ALLISON BLANKENSHIP • TONI L. BOYLES • ANNE F. CRAIGS
LAURIE GUEST • CINDY KUBICA • NANCY J. LEWIS
ANN E. MAH • SARITA MAYBIN • SUSAN MEYER-MILLER
HEIDI RICHARDS • JANIS E. STEWART • CYNTHIA B. STOTLAR
VICKI TREMBLY • DJ WATSON

The Indispensable Guidebook
for Women in the Workplace!

MaroCom Publishing Company

For information contact:
MaroCom Publishing Company
PO Box 9492
Tyler, Texas 75711-9492
1-800-304-5758
Email: info@MaroCom.com
Web: www.MaroCom.com

ISBN # 0-9704592-6-2
FIRST EDITION

Quality MaroCom™ Books

Career Compass for Women:
The Indispensible Guidebook for Women in the Workplace!

The Service Path:
Your Roadmap For Building Strong Customer Loyalty!

The Leadership Path:
Your Roadmap For Leading People In The 21st Century!

The Productivity Path:
Your Roadmap For Improving Employee Performance!

The Communication Path:
Your Roadmap For Building Rapport And Getting Ideas Across!

The Wellness Path:
Your Roadmap For Living Healthy And Feeling Great!

The Teambuilding Path:
Your Roadmap for Creating Highly Productive Teams!

TABLE OF CONTENTS

TABLE OF CONTENTS

INTRODUCTION

Career Compass for Women is about women helping women succeed in the workplace. This "guidebook" was written for you by members of the American Business Women's Association who are also professional speakers, trainers, authors, or publishers. It provides a compass for career success and strategies you can put to work today. Each chapter is a "mini-workshop" full of thought-provoking ideas to help you take stock of your business skills.

Career Compass follows a long tradition of business education for women. When Hilary Bufton, Jr., founded the American Business Women's Association in 1949, the purpose was to bring together women of diverse backgrounds to learn business skills. He recognized that to be successful in the workplace required lifelong learning. In the early years, the members broke new ground by simply daring to meet together in the evenings!

Now, we break new ground again by sharing our expertise with working women everywhere. We have included contact information for each co-author on the first page of her chapter. Most provide additional services and can be reached through their websites. At the back of the book, you will also find listings of other resources available from the co-authors including books, tapes, and programs.

I hope you find this book enjoyable as well as helpful to your career. In it we share our stories and tips for success the same way that women have always shared their stories.

The Best of Success to You!

Ann Mah
Co-Author & Series Editor
Owner – Discover! Strategies
ABWA 2002 National President

PS: For information about ABWA, visit www.abwa.org

PPS: For information about the complete *"Compass Series for Women,"* visit www.CompassSeries.com

CHAPTER ONE

Real Women Have Chipped Nails

How to live an imperfect life and love it!

Allison Adams Blankenship

Real Life…Real Solutions…Real Fun! is the message in every keynote and seminar with Allison Blankenship. She's been described as a speaker who can reach both heads and hearts.

Combining practical, easy-to-use, hands-on tools with boundless energy, Allison delivers content-rich programs that are fun and entertaining. Her experience includes a 20-year award-winning career in corporate communications with clients in finance, banking, retail, hospitality, tourism, insurance and healthcare.

In 1996, she founded the Enrichment Center of Southwest Florida, Inc., a motivation management company in Naples, Florida. Allison speaks across the country 150 times a year on strengthening communications, overcoming conflict and reducing stress.

Allison's audiences applaud her home-style humor, sensible strategies and easy-to-apply ideas. She weaves real-life examples of being a successful business professional, consultant, speaker and step-mom of two teenagers throughout her presentations while giving participants the tools and techniques they need to succeed.

Enrichment Center of Southwest Florida, Inc.
Naples, FL • 800-664-7641 • www.AllisonSpeaks.com

Allison Adams Blankenship

Real Women Have Chipped Nails

How to have an imperfect life and love it!

Do you try to schedule 80 hours in a day instead of eight? Do you ever get depressed when it is time to relax? Have you ever put off a project waiting for more time or the "perfect" time to complete it? Do you make time for everyone else but not for yourself? If so, welcome to the world of perfection.

THE PROBLEM WITH PERFECTION

Joe Gilliam, author of *The Winner in You*, once said that men tackle obstacles outside themselves to be successful. On the other hand, women battle themselves as enemies on the path to prosperity. Throughout a 20-year communications career, I also found that my biggest challenges were internal – my need to perform versus the need to be "perfect."

The problem with perfection is that nobody wins. According to Monica Ramirez Basco, author of *Never Good Enough*, perfection takes a toll in many areas of life:

- It keeps you from succeeding or being happy

- It sets unreal expectations

- You never have enough time

Perfectionism plagues both men and women although career-oriented women seem to be extremely susceptible. We feel guilty for neglecting our family and loved ones and then overcompensate.

Or, we constantly push ourselves to improve, creating emotional stress for everyone around us.

That was my situation. At age 30, I reached a career pinnacle. After one year of work in an industry where I had no previous experience, I was named regional director. I was both exhilarated and terrified. As a result, I pushed myself beyond my physical capacity and ignored the warning signs.

Looking back, I realize that I tried to prove to myself and everyone else that I deserved this promotion. Unfortunately, I was the only one who needed convincing. When my self-confidence wavered, I spiraled into deep depression. The "black hole" was so cavernous and infinite that it seemed there would never be relief. For the first time, I understood how people find the will to end their lives.

This depression was a wake-up call after a lifetime of overachieving. Within the last decade, I've assembled tools to make the most of time and talents, end procrastination and allow more time to truly enjoy life. "Life is what happens when you make other plans," noted John Lennon. In this case, life is what happens when you choose priorities over perfection.

PRIORITIES, NOT PERFECTION

In *The Contented Achiever*, Don Hutson said, "You can't manage time, you can only manage activities that consume time." One myth to conquer is the idea that there is more time later to complete projects "perfectly." Each day has 24 hours – no more, no less. As Hutson says, we must harness the power of each minute and give up waiting for more time.

"But," you say, "I haven't enough time to get it all done!" That is true. But you do have a way to sort out which tasks are most worthy of your time and energy. It starts with a brain download.

Have you ever awakened in panic in the middle of the night? Your brain screams, "Emergency!" because you just remembered something you forgot to do. It's doubtful you'll go back to sleep unless you write the task down.

Write it down, make it happen

Writing down urgent to-dos and messages allows your mind to move from remembering data to problem solving. There is a direct correlation between writing goals and accomplishing them. Yet according to a study by Harvard University, only 3% of the population writes down this information.

The first step to determine how to best use your time is to create a to-do list. Just dump all thoughts, want-to-dos, should-dos and have-to-dos on paper. Don't try to organize it yet. The goal is to transfer it from your mind to paper.

So many choices, so little time

Once you've written your list, separate personal vs. professional tasks. Keeping two distinct lists eliminates some guilt and stress. The first items on most people's lists are the most emotional or urgent. Your goal is to determine which activities are worthy of your focus and energy.

Traditional prioritizing tools often result in five or six #1 priorities a day. The following Priority Scale Indicator is a helpful resource to decide which is your single top priority. If you are a linear thinker, you do this naturally. You can use this scale to teach others how to organize their time and thoughts.

Write your most important priorities in the blanks below, one item per line. Continue listing tasks until you have filled in each blank below.

1._____					
2._____	1/2				
3._____	1/3	2/3			
4._____	1/4	2/4	3/4		
5._____	1/5	2/5	3/5	4/5	
6._____	1/6	2/6	3/6	4/6	5/6

Once your list is complete, compare each activity individually – that is what the "fractions", or ratios, to right of the blanks indicate. "1/2" actually means activity #1 compared to #2. Be brutally honest. Ask yourself "If I only have time for one of the two, which is more important?" Not urgent – important. If it is number one, circle number one in the ratio, and so forth.

Compare each item in the list, each time circling the number of the activity that is more important.

Below is a sample of the finished product:
1. Check email
2. Outline PowerPoint slides   1/②
3. Call client   1/③ ②/3
4. Lunch with Jim   1/④ ②/4 3/④
5. Order new business cards   1/⑤ ②/5 3/⑤ 4/⑤
6. Finish rough draft   1/⑥ 2/⑥ 3/⑥ 4/⑥ 5/⑥

To determine your new priority order, count the number of times each number was circled. The number with the highest vote is the number one priority. In this case, that number is circled five times, or #6. Proceed to the next highest, four, etc. The Priority Scale Indicator can include 15 items. There is always a descending order for the number of blanks. In this example, the order is 5,4,3,2,1,0.

A tied score is easy to resolve. Since you need a descending order, simply choose between the two tied priorities. One becomes more important than the other, completing your descending order. For example, if you are tied with two #3 activities, you'll have a 5, 2, 1, and 0. You need a 4 and a 3. Decide which of the two #3 activities is more important – that priority becomes the 4 and the other remains a 3. You now have 5,4,3,2,1,0.

What happens when the first activity gets the big fat zero but you are stressed about it? That happened at a women's leadership conference where I spoke. A woman volunteered her list of activities. The first activity listed was "clean out the basement." It wasn't hard to see that the basement was going to score zero. She refused to believe it and insisted we do the activity over. We did – three times. Each time, guess what got the big fat zero? The basement!

Amazingly, the woman got angry with me, blaming me for not being able to make the basement a #1 priority. She refused to accept the idea that the first items we list are more urgent than important. Another volunteer shared a story about cleaning her basement that provided the perfect example of our next tool.

One step at a time...

The second volunteer said that she also needed to clean the basement, but wasn't inspired by the thought of spending hours cleaning. She used a kitchen timer. Every time she loaded her washing machine, she set the timer for 5, 10 or 15 minutes. During that time, she sorted through her basement, weeding out trash and charitable items. When the timer rang, she decided whether to continue for another round or go about her business. This is a perfect example of the *Law of the Slight Edge: Small things, over time, make a big difference.*

The Slight Edge has limitless uses. I use it to keep my yard neat. I used to spend 20-30 minutes every morning pulling weeds on my way to pick up the newspaper. When I applied the Slight Edge by filling a small plastic shopping bag with weeds, it only took 10 minutes. It also gave me the satisfaction of pulling an entire bag of weeds. The yard looked great and I "saved" 10-20 minutes daily.

Consider the following chart describing the cumulative effect of lost or wasted minutes:

Minutes per Day	Minutes per Week	Hours per Year	8-hour Days per Year
5	35	30	3.8
15	105	90	11.4
30	210	182	22.8
60	420	364	45.5

This chart demonstrates the power of five minutes a day. Many people don't have time to exercise or go to a gym. But they do have five minutes a day to park further away or take the stairs. That five minutes may not seem like much but by the end of year, you've "exercised" almost four full business days – do you think that will make a difference to your weight and energy? Absolutely!

At work, the Slight Edge can make a major difference, too. Keep 5-10-15 minute folders. Drop tasks, emails, articles to read and phone messages into the files based on the amount of time needed. Then, when you need a quick break or are waiting for a meeting to start, pull out one of these brief tasks. You will be amazed at how much you accomplish throughout the day.

Now you can make smart choices with three tools: the brain download list, the Priority Scale Indicator and the Law of the Slight Edge. Yet, what happens when your best intentions go out the window in a heartbeat? It's called the "but first" disease…

JUST DO IT! ENDING PROCRASTINATION

It's the weekend and you need to do the laundry. In the hallway near the laundry room, you spot the morning paper on the coffee table. "I'll do the laundry," you say to yourself, "BUT FIRST I'll just pick up those papers." Reaching for the paper, you notice the coffee mug. "Okay," you say. "I'll pick up the papers BUT FIRST I'll just put this in the sink." You walk into the kitchen with the mug and notice the remote control. "What's that doing in here? I'll put the cup away BUT FIRST I'll put the remote back." By the end of the day, the laundry still needs to be done, the papers are still on the table, the coffee cup isn't washed and the remote is missing. You can't figure out why because you KNOW you were busy all day!

Time's Up!

Remember the kitchen timer? It also helps end procrastination. We put off doing tasks and chores that we don't like, don't have enough time to do "right" or are boring. Unfortunately, leaving incomplete tasks creates immense stress. Everything piles up and nothing gets done.

Starting a task is usually the hardest step. That's where a timer is so useful. You may set the timer for any amount of time. Just give yourself (and others) permission to quit when the timer goes off. Then decide whether to continue. Most of the time, I go a few extra rounds and put a good dent in the task. Using a timer is an excellent way to teach young children and teens to help around the house. They know the chore is tangible and won't take all day.

The business version is to use the timer on your PDA or Microsoft Outlook. It is especially helpful to get rid of office pests who want to hang out and chat. Your timer goes off, signaling that you have a "pressing" appointment – with yourself, of course!

How do you eat an elephant? One bite at a time!

I acquired my second favorite procrastination-buster quite by accident. After we moved into our new home in the woods, I left the garage door open on a chilly night. The next morning, I discovered an overnight "guest" – a baby raccoon. Hissing and spitting, the raccoon scurried about the garage, hiding behind boxes and cars. Although the woods were less than 50 feet away, the animal refused to take refuge there.

Then it dawned on me. Those 50 feet were open unprotected space. Animals instinctively know not to enter open unprotected areas. I placed a box a few feet outside the garage. Immediately, the raccoon ran to the box. Then I placed a second box behind the first. When I lifted the first box, the animal ran to the second. We leap-frogged boxes all the way across the opening until the animal was safe.

Many times tasks are like those woods – we know we need to get there but the process seems overwhelming. Like the boxes, you can break the tasks into small, manageable pieces. Combine small steps with your timer and that task is done quickly.

Make it fun

Sometimes you just have to humor yourself to find the motivation to start a project. Using rewards or making a task fun is a great way to bribe yourself. Don't laugh – it works! Whenever I get writer's block, I put on a sequined tiara at my desk. It makes me laugh, gets me out of my rut and helps me refocus. (The Fed Ex man thinks I'm nuts, but who cares?!) Or I reward myself with a walk, a snack, etc.

Making the chore fun is the best way to create buy-in from others. When my children were little, I needed to clean leftovers from the refrigerator. One night, I set all the leftovers out like a buffet line and put four numbers in a bowl. Everybody drew a number. Whoever drew #1 went through the line first and chose whatever they wanted to eat – all desserts was okay. The goal was to get rid of food. "Leftover Lotto" was an instant hit. Ten years later, my kids still ask for it.

You need buy-in at work to accomplish unpleasant tasks. Look for simple, creative ways to make it fun. We schedule one Friday a month where everyone wears jeans to clean out the file room. It is surprising how something so small makes such a difference in attitude.

THE POWER OF LETTING GO

Living and loving an imperfect life is very simple when you focus on a key ingredient: attitude. It is easy to believe that everything we do is important. Unfortunately, it isn't. A friend shared a terrific way to stop taking on the world's problems. She carries a Q-Tip in her purse or pocket at all times. Q-Tip stands for: Quit Taking It Personally.

Every time she finds herself giving in to unrealistic expectations or guilt, she remembers the Q-Tip. "It's not my job to run the world – although I'd be very good at it!" she once told me. The same is true for you. It is not your job to make everyone happy, or feel good about themselves or like each other. Your job is to determine which priorities are truly important and worthy of your time and attention.

Once you conquer the need to perform vs. be perfect, you find you make worthy choices. You invest time in yourself without guilt. You become proactive in accomplishing tasks and more realistic with your time commitments. The goal is not to be perfect; it is about being excellent. After all, nobody's perfect — real women have chipped nails!

CHAPTER TWO

Stop the World, I Want to Get Off

Or...how to survive difficult situations.

Toni L. Boyles

Toni Boyles is "WANTED" for making people Laugh, Learn & Celebrate Life. Toni is a National Speaker, Trainer, Business Owner (the most exciting retreat center in the world), Mother, World Traveler, Wife, Friend, Daughter, Sister, Creative Thinker, Humorist and Real Person.

She is "GUILTY" of making people participate, laugh, cry, work and think. Her favorite weapons include humor, personal stories, interactive participation, skills practice and more. She actually believes "People can change." and "Learning that brings about no change is as effective as a parachute that opens on the first bounce." She will do almost anything to facilitate learning.

Toni has over 19 years experience in training on a variety of topics. She is a graduate of Washburn University with a BA in Communications. Before starting her own training company, Boyles worked as a Staff Development Specialist for the Kansas Department of Transportation. Toni and her husband David recently remodeled a historic 1928 brick and stone building to serve as a training and retreat center. The facility is located in Tecumseh, KS and is called "A Place in Time." Toni lives in Tecumseh with her husband. They have two adult children and three wonderful grandchildren.

A Place In Time
Tecumseh, KS • 785-379-8463 • www.aplaceintimeonline.com

Toni L. Boyles

Stop the World, I Want to Get Off

Or...how to survive difficult situations.

Very few things in my life do I remember as clearly as the opening line to *The Road Less Traveled* by M. Scott Peck. It made a huge impact on my thinking. Life is difficult. Three simple words, yet some of the most truthful ever written. The message that followed was basically "Get over it". Do you know anyone who does not have difficulties? Think of a time when you struggled to get past a problem. Was it the end of your problems, or were there more? Maybe the next one was even more difficult. To have problems and difficult situations is to be alive. You are in good company.

Experience and the counsel of many wise people taught me several practices to use in handling difficult situations. None of them contain magic, but they are very powerful. They are options that will lead to a more well-balanced, productive life.

No two situations are alike and no one practice will work all the time. It may be necessary to use several with any given situation. You will have the opportunity to practice them at work and in your personal life. That is why I call them practices, not strategies. The more you apply them to every part of your life, the more you will own them. They are 24 / 7 ways of thinking.

Think back on recent difficult situations you have had. It might have been other people, equipment or Mother Nature. Something is always offering you the chance to see the strength of your character.

Reading about how to deal with difficult situations will not by itself make any improvement in your skills. Promise yourself to try the ideas at the end of each practice. Here we go!

TAKE CHARGE, MAKE THE RIGHT CHOICE...

Have you ever said, "He made me do it"? Or maybe you said, "It makes me so upset." The truth is, people and events cannot control us unless we give our permission. You are in charge of your behavior. It is one of the most powerful things you own. We give away that power when we respond with emotions. The irony is that most often we give our power to people at whom we're angry or to things we don't like.

In each situation where you feel stress or anxiety, say over and over to yourself before you respond, "I have two choices." The choices are "to make it better or to make it worse." It would be wonderful to be able to fix things or people, but none of the world's scholars have figured that one out. The thing we all own is the ability to choose based on what we value. That choice will make things better.

This practice is one I developed several years ago while researching material for a management training course. Even though this is an age-old truism, I credit the book Seven Habits of Highly Effective People by Dr. Stephen Covey for allowing me to finally get it. Not until you hand your power over to others can they control you. Which will it be? Make it better or make it worse, your choice. Covey did not give that to me and I'm not giving it to you. Or as the group AMERICA so eloquently put it. "Oz never did give nothing to the Tin Man that he didn't, didn't already have." You own that power. Choose to use it. Plan your actions based on your values.

Write the words "I am in charge –I have two choices". Post it somewhere you will see often. Keep a journal of the times you felt in charge of your behavior and also the times you gave away your choices. Reflect on how you would have liked to respond.

LOOK IN THE MIRROR...

You've made the choice to use what you value instead of emotions to make things better. Great. Now you need to find a big mirror. The mirror is symbolic but it has tremendous power. Take a good honest look at yourself. What role did you play in the situation? What share of the responsibility was yours? What could you have done differently? Using this practice on a regular basis will allow you to learn self-correction. Look long and hard at yourself every day. Part of doing this effectively is to ask someone you trust to offer his or her reflection. It is critical to allow them to speak freely without fear. In life everything is a dance and you are dancing, too. Look at your dance carefully. Your behavior may be the one that needs to change. If so, great. You can control that.

Identify a person you trust and ask them to be your mirror.
Research The Johari Window. Learn all you can about the Blind Self.
Trust me, it is important.

SEE THE BIG PICTURE...

You have begun the process of seeing the Big Picture by looking in the mirror. However, that is not nearly enough. My observation is that we are conditioned to think in the short term and to make decisions based on little information. An obvious practice would be to gather information. Do not respond to situations until you have as much information as possible. Sometimes there is very little information to be found. In that case, learn to ask yourself, "What is it I do not know? What else might be going on?" When we can open our minds to the "what ifs" out there, we make better choices. Doing this will not fix problems, but it will offer you more choices and may just keep your foot out of your mouth.

There is a story about my husband I'd like to share. He is a wonderful man that I consider to be a "9 ½" most of the time. He does however have just a few developmental needs. One of them has to do with his driving attitude. Driving to him is a difficult situation. I call his behavior behind the wheel of a car "cussing and grumbling." No one can drive as well as he can. Everyone is too slow, too fast or just in his way. After reading an article reinforcing the Big Picture theory I tried to share it with him. He was not interested and I knew my attempt had fallen on deaf ears. As a trainer I know that a teachable moment will make all the difference. I waited for just the right time. It did not take long.

We were driving late at night out in the country with no traffic, when I noticed a car sitting dead still at the stop sign in front of us. It came, just like always. Cuss and grumble... grumble and cuss. I decided to jump at the chance. "Now David," I said. "You do not know what is going on in that car". The person could have spilled coffee and is cleaning it up, or they may have lost their directions and are reading the map, or they may not be feeling well. Ask yourself what else might be happening to them and drive around without all the grumbling." Again it seemed that my point was wasted. He did drive around them, but grumbled all the way.

Words in the car are usually followed by silence. This time was no different. As we rode along in silence I found myself thinking what a poor trainer I was. I thought I'd offered such a good example! It was David who broke the silence. He leaned over to me and with sarcasm declared, "Or maybe the guy's wife was nagging at him!" I was thrilled! He had gotten the message loud and clear after all. I must admit that as thrilled as I was with his understanding of the Big Picture concept, I think there may have been an insult intended.

The next time a co-worker or customer yells at you, ask yourself several Big Picture questions. What else may be going on with them? Is it really me they are upset with?

UNDERSTAND DIFFERENCES IN OTHERS...

No description of this practice, just a simple assignment.
Read the chapter in this book by Cindy Kubica about different personalities and temperaments. It is critically important in dealing with people who think differently than you.

ASK YOURSELF, "WHAT IS HALF OF EIGHT"?...

Do you know the answer? Maybe the question should be "How many answers do you know?" Write them down. I'll wait. Have you done it? How many did you get? Did you get three, ten, twenty, or fifty? I'm not sure I know how many there are, but there are at least fifty. I ask this question often in class to see how far out of the box people can get. Most of the time a group will get five or six but not more than ten. I'll even add answers to the list but they often do not understand them.

By now you are asking, "What does this have to do with difficult situations?" One of the most important things in dealing with difficult situations is to think of multiple solutions. Often things seem difficult because we fail to consider more than one or two options. I do not believe the world is black and white. There are options you have not been open enough to explore. Remember to ask yourself, "What is the other half of eight." Or is it ate?

Keep working on the question. Check out the page on my web site (aplaceintimeonline.com) that says Half of ???. If you know more, send me an email with your answers.

REFRAME SITUATIONS...

When I was nineteen I got my first speeding ticket. I was scared to death. I just knew my social life was over. My dad would be furious. I was crying hysterically while the officer was trying his best to calm me. I remember his words to this day. "A ticket is so much better than a wreck." He repeated it over and over. Little did I know how much wisdom he was offering. Whenever you are faced with what seems to be a difficult situation, try to keep it in perspective. Reframe the picture. Ask yourself; will this matter in a year, six months, a week, or an hour? How important is it anyway? Is it worth my physical and mental health? What is the worst thing that can happen and can I handle it? Rarely does the worst happen and even then most things can be survived.

Go to the library and find my favorite story about reframing situations. It is short, funny and powerful. It is on page 143 in the paperback version of UH OH by Robert Fulghrum. I know you will love Sigmund Wollman as I do after reading this story.

RE-LEARN TO LAUGH...

Babies prove we have the power to laugh early in life, but many of us unlearned this powerful skill as we grew into responsible adults. C.W. Metcalf calls it "Terminal Professionalism". I am suggesting you "re-learn to laugh". Find humor in your life every day. Develop the ability to access humor in the midst of adversity.

One of the most requested workshops I offer is "Humor in the

Workplace". As part of that workshop I ask people to share stories about using humor in difficult situations. They have filled my heart and head full of stories. I could write a book with only that as a topic. The theme is obvious. There are many times when you must laugh or lose your sanity. A majority of stories are about hospitals and funerals. Things generally do not get more difficult than that.

Humor is a skill you can develop just like any other. It can empower you in many ways. It keeps things in perspective, lowers your stress and allows you to communicate more effectively. There is a major difference in childish and child- like behavior. Imagine how different the world would be if everyone took humor seriously. What if we all considered it a major responsibility? It is a choice you can work on every day.

Build a humor collection. Books, Articles, Cartoons, Friends. Collect whatever will help you develop this skill.

FIND GOOD RESOURCES...

During problem-solving workshops, I give participants a page of puzzles and ask them to solve them in two minutes. After two minutes I allow them to find a partner and continue. Next they join another pair and work as a team of four. The last thing I offer is the option to ask anyone in the room for help. Without fail people are more successful when they allow others to help them. It is a great truism in life. Problems shared are more easily figured out. There are other learning points here. If I ask them later where they got their first partner they will tell me it was the person sitting closest to them. Don't we do that in real life? When we do ask for help it is not always from someone who might know the most. It is simply the first person we can find. Also, 99% of the time no one will come to me. I stand at the front of the room with the answers in my hand. Remember I offered anyone in the room. We are our own worst enemy when we limit our resources.

Select a problem you have been working on. Find someone who is familiar with it and together brainstorm who and what your resources are.

PACK EXTRA BATTERIES...

This practice is intended to keep those difficult situations at bay. It is always better to avoid them when you can. The first time I really connected to this concept was at a camp retreat center and my equipment would not work because the batteries were dead. All the problem solving and positive thinking in the world did not help. If only I had packed extra batteries. I have also heard this practice referred to as "give yourself room to breathe". There are hundreds of ways you can do this.

- Leave an extra 10 minutes early for appointments

- Build trust with co-workers before conflicts occurs

- Never let the gas gauge get below half full

- Always carry an extra pair of panty hose in the car

- Keep a casserole in the freezer at all times

- Carry extra batteries or light bulbs for equipment

In other words plan for things to go wrong and allow for a back up. It feels really good to know you have plenty of room to breathe.

When things go wrong, develop the habit of asking yourself, "How could I have allowed myself more room to breathe?" It is surprising how often you know the answer and how simple it may be to do.

A FINAL THOUGHT...

This list of practices is not a complete list. Your final assignment is to find people you respect and ask them. "What is your counsel when it comes to dealing with difficult situations?" Then listen, learn, practice and pass the information on to others. Life is difficult. However it is also Awesome.

Keep Laughing Learning and Celebrating Life!

NOTES:

CHAPTER THREE

The 4 Keys to Smart Hiring

Straightforward advice from the front lines.

Anne F. Craigs

As the new century began, Anne F. Craigs was reinventing herself. She went from being a senior manager at a mid-sized savings bank in the northeast to an entrepreneur and is now co-owner of three ventures, The Employment Times, A&J Consulting and Craigs & Paquette, LLC.

Anne derives most of her management experience from banking and finance. As a senior bank officer, Anne was responsible for branch administration, strategic planning and marketing. But never one to let moss grow under her feet, she and her business partner, Jeanne S. Paquette, worked to create an entirely new venture, which has now grown into three new businesses.

The adventure began with *The Employment Times*, which was born out of the belief that companies needed more expertise in recruiting the best candidates. "We offer a combination of management, human resources, marketing and planning to help Human Resources professionals recruit more effectively."

Anne and Jeanne work with companies to provide recruitment marketing and seminars on various employment topics including recruitment, marketing and supervision.

The Employment Times
Auburn, ME • 866-657-5444 • www.employmenttimesonline.com

<u>Anne F. Craigs</u>

The 4 Keys to Smart Hiring

Straightforward advice from the front lines.

The new retail outlet needed to hire 12 people to open the store. They had only 4 weeks to hire everyone. Hiring this number of people would be especially difficult in the market where unemployment was running at 3%. When unemployment is that low, there are few people available in the market place who are not already working. They would have to entice workers from their current jobs.

They ran an ad in the local Sunday classified section and, as difficult as the market was, they were able to hire all 12 people by the deadline. The store opened on time. The store manager was congratulated by the district manager for pulling off such a wonderful success. Sales were robust and everyone was excited about the possibilities of success and the promise of future bonuses.

Within 3 months, all 12 employees had left the store. Sales declined due to poor customer service. The store manager had to take on more and more hours and was suffering from burn-out. The district manager was getting pressure from the corporate office to improve sales and he put pressure on the store manager and remaining employees. By the end of the first year, the store had gained a reputation for poor service. Sales declined further. The economy slipped. The corporate office thought the location was not meeting its expectations and blamed market conditions for declining sales. In an effort to cut their losses, they worked with a competitor to take over the location.

What went wrong? It could have been a poor location or the economy, but more likely there was a fundamental issue at the root of the problem. They hired the wrong people to carry out the mission of the new store.

All the right marketing, all the best research and business consulting, can be a giant waste of time (and money) if they are placed in the hands of the wrong group of employees. Every manager or business owner wants to believe that they can pick out the best from a crowd of applicants. Indeed, their success as owners and managers depends upon attracting good people to carry out the corporate mission.

Over time, the science of recruiting has taken over the art of the function. Companies have moved toward personality and ethics tests as a way of ferreting out the character of the candidates they interview. They put less reliance on their own intuition than on the results from a bubble test. There is definitely an art to picking the best candidates and motivating them to succeed. Recruiting is like any other skill. Hiring managers get better at selecting good candidates the more they are able to engage in the recruiting process.

The hiring manager of the retail outlet made the fatal error of believing that anyone could do the jobs. Hiring managers need to know the fundamentals of the entire process. Recruiting looks simple, but companies that treat the process as simplistic do so at their peril.

Recruiting is expensive. It is much more costly than the expenses shown on the financial statements. Some are hard-dollar costs. These are the expenses surrounding the advertising, the head hunter fees, the internet web site recruiting contracts, etc. The retail outlet believed that these were the only costs. They ran one ad and hired 12 people. Sounds cost effective. However, the loss of a retail location to a competitor has many costs beyond the expense of one ad. There is much more that lurks under the surface.

The cost of losing a good employee can be as much as three times their annual salary. Not all of this expense is visible. It can take several weeks, even months, to find qualified candidates for some positions. Companies cannot grow when key positions go unfilled. These are the "soft" costs of turnover. No one really notices them on a financial report because they are represented not by what is stated in the numbers, but what is missing from them. They are opportunities and revenue that never get the chance to appear on the income statement versus expenses that can be tallied in a neat column.

There are 4 Keys to Smart Hiring:

- Job analysis
- Marketing the position
- Interviewing process
- Orientation

By using the four keys to recruit and retain employees, you will be giving your company an advantage in the highly competitive job market.

KEY #1: JOB ANALYSIS

Assume your company has a position to fill. The first step is NOT to dash to the newspaper or internet to run an ad. Begin instead by asking yourself, is the job I need to fill the same one that is being vacated? If the position has been filled for some time, chances are the job has evolved.

First, look at the job description and compare it to the actual function being performed. Is this the job you WANT to fill? Do you NEED to fill this job at all? Determine if the position is needed, and if so, what skills does it take to do the job well. By doing this type of review, you will find that you may need some formal reorganization of the department, or that the informal reorganization has already taken place and you simply need to acknowledge it.

As you let this process play out, you will most likely develop the beginnings of a candidate profile (assuming your analysis leads you to believe the position must be filled). By talking to co-workers and exploring the needs of the company, you can determine the characteristics of a successful candidate.

KEY #2: MARKETING THE JOB

Finding and hiring the right candidate is very similar to the "lead generation" process used by sales people. Your network of contacts is an extremely valuable asset when filling a position. Even when you have no openings, it is important to continue to cultivate a rich network of contacts. Your contacts may reveal candidates, but more likely, they will lead you to meet others who may fill the needs of the company.

It is important not to ignore the network opportunities in your own company. Begin with current employees. Your good employees probably have friends and colleagues who are also good employees. By developing a referral program for existing employees to refer potential candidates to the Human Resources Department, you will be cultivating a potential recruiting bonanza.

However, not all networking efforts pay off with perfect candidates for every position. Other methods must be used to enrich the pool of candidates. Use a variety of tools including classified advertising in newspapers, trade magazines, your own company web site, a career web site, a job hotline, radio and television, to name a few of the more popular ones. Whatever method you prefer, consider using as many of the outlets as your budget allows. Remember, this is a marketing project.

When selecting the medium for your message, consider the candidate profile you have developed. Where will that candidate look for a position? If the position is for a truck driver, s/he is more than likely not using a computer during the work day. Since most people search for their next job while at work, the truck driver ad needs to be where truck drivers will see or hear it - in newspaper classified advertising, or if the budget allows, on the radio.

Recruitment advertising is really no different than other marketing messages. The reach and frequency of the message will determine how many people hear and see the message. You must decide how often the message needs to be seen/heard and by how many people. Also, the right mix of media (ie, radio and billboard, newspaper, trade paper) will help put your message in front of the people you need to attract.

If the position is difficult to fill and there are limited qualified candidates, then you will need a greater geographic reach and more frequent message to successfully hire the right person. If the position is extremely desirable, you may not need to advertise at all. Your highly developed network may be your best resource.

If print advertising is necessary, then there are a few things to consider. First is your company image. Every marketing message, even those contained in help-wanted advertisements either add or detract from your company image. Your ad will be seen by your current employees, vendors, and customers as well as potential candidates. A well-crafted recruitment ad should enhance your image in the minds of all those groups.

Your logo is necessary, not optional. Look at the other marketing materials your company uses and make the recruitment ad consistent with the look already established. The ad should contain some information about your company or its mission. The emotional content of the ad is important. Changing jobs is a "big ticket purchase" for both the employee and the employer. Emotions are a major element that will guide much of the decision.

The job title should be prominent in the ad and should be a title that people recognize. Confusing job titles will keep some qualified candidates from applying. If you are looking for a bookkeeper and you advertise the need for a four-year degree, then is it really an accounting position? Accountants will read "bookkeeper," consider the position beneath their skill level and not apply. Bookkeepers will apply, but will be unqualified. The result is that the position remains unfilled for longer than the company can afford and the Human Resources Department looks like it is not doing its job. No one wins.

Other important content for the ad includes the qualifications needed and the requirements of the position. These can be short descriptions, but refrain from abbreviations to save space. Abbreviated words take more time to read and interpret. If you use too many, you will lose the interest of your reader.

The size and design of your ad will send a message also. When you advertise for a senior position, the ad size must match the value of the position. To recruit a Vice President of Finance, the ad must be large and prominent. Why? Because a VP of Finance is an important position, and these people do not look in the line ads of the classified section of the newspaper for their next position. They are networking, searching on the internet, reading the trade publications and other targeted periodicals. If you are not advertising in these same places and networking in the same circles, then you will not attract the best candidate for your company. Cast a wide net and you will be rewarded with good applicants from which to choose.

KEY #3: INTERVIEWING

Now you have attracted a pool of applicants. The next key is interviewing. When you are at the point of interviewing candidates for the position, consider involving several people from the company. Of course, you must make sure the interviewers are qualified and prepared to be a part of the process. A review of the legal aspects of hiring would be prudent to make certain you are in compliance with the Equal Employment laws and regulations. Make sure everyone involved in the interviewing process understands the hiring process at your company and knows the timeline involved in this hire. By keeping everyone informed, you avoid confusion and look like a company that "has it all together."

Prior to the interview, be sure to familiarize yourself with the candidate's resume. Make notes about anything you especially want to ask about. Red flags on resumes include vague position descriptions or job titles; gaps between jobs need attention. During the interview, you will want to know the circumstances of the candidate's departure from each job.

The interview is supposed to reveal how well the candidate matches the job requirements and the company culture. As the interviewer, consider yourself the company host/hostess. You will want to make the candidate comfortable with some small talk. Not only is this a polite way to introduce new people to the company, but candidates often reveal information about themselves in small talk that is important to know.

The interview needs to be held in a private setting. No interruptions, no phone calls. The candidate deserves your undivided attention. Feel free to take notes during the conversation. You will have difficulty keeping all the candidate information clear in your mind once you have interviewed several people. Make notes that will help you to remember the candidate, but be careful not to write down anything that would be construed as discriminatory.

Getting into the questions you have about the candidate's background can sometimes be awkward. Consider having the candidate begin with a "verbal resume." This will let the candidate emphasize areas s/he considers important. You can observe body language and voice intonation. As the candidate speaks freely, s/he will give you clues about attitude, impressions of his/her previous managers and employers. You may get information that would not have come up otherwise.

Follow up with questions. Most questions should be open-ended unless you are verifying facts. For example, an open-ended question would be: "What did your previous manager do to make your job so unpleasant that you felt you had to leave?" versus a closed-ended question that can be answered with a simple "yes" or "no": "Your previous manager was difficult to work with?" In the end, the candidate should have done more talking than the interviewer, but do not let the candidate leave without a review of the job requirements, the hiring time-line, and how you will follow-up with him/her.

Once the interviews are concluded, it is time to make a decision. Be sure to ask for feedback from all those who participated in the process either individually or in a group, but understand that the final decision must be made by one person. A "consensus candidate" often is not the best candidate, but simply the one that threatens the fewest number of people. A dangerous trap.

Your company may use a personality test and/or a skills test. These are important devices, but should never take the place of a real decision. They are guides for hiring managers, not substitutes.

After the final candidates have been chosen and tested, remember to check the candidate's references. Reference checking may not provide much information other than the hire date, but it is still a good idea to get references on your final choices. Don't waste time on personal references, but you can often get into a conversation with a previous supervisor or subordinate that is enlightening. Even silence speaks volumes. You will not always be rewarded with a rich source of information, but ignoring the references can come back to haunt you. Remember to get written consent from applicants to contact previous professional references before you begin.

It is important to remember to communicate with all the applicants who sent you resumes. Though time consuming, remind yourself that all of these people are potential customers, vendors or future employees. If you drop the ball at this point, you have minimized your image in their minds. When you have only a few people, telephone them and explain that you have hired another candidate.

When there is an abundance of applicants, it is wise to send a postcard as soon as you receive their resume. It can simply say that you have received their resume and will contact them if they are chosen for an interview. No further follow up is necessary for anyone other than the final candidates. As difficult as the conversation may be, the final candidates should receive the courtesy of a phone call.

KEY #4: ORIENTATION

Now you have offered the position to your first choice. The candidate has been hired, but the recruiting job is not finished yet. It is important that you orient new hires into your company the right way. By giving the first impressions of your company a high priority, you will plant the seeds of a loyal employee. On the first day, you probably have paperwork for the new hire to complete. If you get this done in an environment where you explain the expectations of the company, the paperwork will not seem so mundane.

Give the new person a tour of the facility, even if you only have two offices. Be sure to show them where the restroom, the coffee pot and pencil sharpener are. Even the use of the telephone may seem basic, but every telephone system is different. Give the new hire a little lesson. Explain the courtesies expected by other employees. For people new to the work world, consider assigning a mentor to the new hire so that any question can be answered quickly and easily. Usually it is the little things that create the greatest anxiety for the new hire, not the depths of the position. If you have made arrangements to relieve the new hire from these usual anxieties, your new hire will have a much more comfortable first day and you will have made a good impression.

The keys to smart hiring include analyzing the job, marketing the job, the interviewing process, and orientation of new employees. By putting these practices in place and making them a part of the culture of your organization, you will be well on your way to hiring smart. Good luck!

For more information about recruiting and managing employees effectively, I would recommend finding a copy of *Think Like a Manager: Everything They Didn't Tell You When They Promoted You* written by Roger Fritz and published by Career Press.

CHAPTER FOUR

I Want to See the Jalapeno Coming

A hot recipe for growing your business.

Laurie Guest

Laurie Guest is known for her imaginative ideas and fast-paced, entertaining style. She is experienced in health care administration and marketing and frequently speaks nationwide on topics that tackle today's business needs.

As a member of the National Speakers Association, Laurie speaks to thousands of people each year and clients repeatedly describe her as a dynamic and genuine presenter who exceeds expectations.

The Career Café offers a distinctive menu of programs and resources customized to fit your needs. Our keynotes, workshops and personal coaching sessions are designed to awaken your spirit and provide practical skills that can be used for life.

Career Cafe
DeKalb, IL • 866-977-7325 • www.careercafe.biz

Laurie Guest

I Want to See the Jalapeno Coming

A hot recipe for growing your business.

According to the United States Small Business Association, more than half of new businesses fail within the first four years. This staggering statistic proves there is much more to being a successful entrepreneur than hanging a shingle and unlocking the front door. Be certain you have done a careful job of planning how to attract your target market and keep them for a lifetime.

A deep understanding of your potential customer is the best place to start when trying to grow a company. Oftentimes a business owner mistakenly assumes that everyone who needs their product or service will be aware of their establishment and choose to become a patron.

This chapter poses six challenging questions for business owners. Respond to each query no matter how daunting the task. Force yourself to write down your thoughts. Taking the time to analyze your business while reading this chapter will prove beneficial.

Describe the people who desire your product or service.

- Male ___ %   Female _____%
- Average Age _____
- Approximate income level _____
- Geographical location _____
- Other pertinent factors _____
- Assuming a customer needs or wants your product, why wouldn't they choose to do business with you?

- What other business in a non-compete industry wants to market to the same group?

- In what manner have you invited people to choose you? (i.e. Marketing, personal request, store appearance)

- Can you package your goods or services differently to make them more attractive?

- What makes your business unique and easy to remember?

STOP! Do not even think about continuing this chapter until you have recorded your responses to the questions above. Just thinking about the response is not enough.

DESCRIBE THE PEOPLE WHO DESIRE YOUR PRODUCT OR SERVICE

When asking a business owner who his or her customers are, I am amazed how often the answer is "everyone." NO! Even if you are selling a product that everyone needs, not everyone is in your target market. Many times the customer's gender, age, discretionary income and place of residence are all important factors to be considered when preparing to market your product or service. Taking the time to properly analyze your best customer will make your marketing plan development easier. Review your current marketing efforts and determine if the direction matches your target group. If this task is a struggle for you, consider seeking paid counsel from an advertising agency or public relations firm.

Example: An ophthalmologist was spending thousands of dollars promoting eye surgery to eliminate the need for corrective eyewear. Initially the advertising was designed to appeal to active, sports-minded, thirty-something adults. The response was good but not great. After reviewing the records of all the surgical patients in the practice it was learned that the best candidates for the surgery had the following description: 60% male, average age 42 and an income level of over $50,000. Interestingly enough, patients stated what motivated them the most to choose surgery was the elimination of the daily hassle of wearing glasses and contacts, not the freedom to participate in sports. These facts allowed the medical practice to change the concept behind their advertising and significantly improve the business.

ASSUMING A CUSTOMER NEEDS OR WANTS YOUR PRODUCT, WHY WOULDN'T THEY CHOOSE TO DO BUSINESS WITH YOU?

One of the smartest ways to achieve business success is to figure out why people AREN'T coming to your establishment. Sometimes finding out the true answer can be a challenge or even a bitter pill to swallow.

Example: A landscaping company was determined to build their business. They are extremely nice people, offer a great selection, and are well liked in the community. However, they had developed a reputation of not providing "on-time" delivery. Over the years the company name had become synonymous with "the gardeners who never show up." This was a crucial factor in the lack of growth they were experiencing. Determined to fix the situation, they made it a top priority to return calls and show up as scheduled. But knowing and doing are two different things. Recently, a friend of mine and a long-time client of this landscape company gave up waiting for her lawn maintenance. She decided to call their competitor. It no longer mattered to her how nice they were or how great the selection. She did not have a good experience and so she took her business elsewhere.

Depending on the nature of your business you can determine if you are retaining customers by utilizing follow-up questionnaires, tracking the percent of repeat business from individual customers, or visiting the competition to see how you measure up!

WHAT OTHER BUSINESS IN A NON-COMPETE INDUSTRY YEARN FOR THE SAME GROUP YOU ARE TARGETING?

Usually a potential customer must encounter a business name multiple times before choosing to do business. The encounter can be achieved through advertising, word of mouth, drive-by attention or media exposure. Many business owners mistakenly believe "if you build it, they will come." Strategic promotion is a must. Finding ways to put your business name at the top of mind awareness will increase your odds of being chosen. One way is to find another business that seeks the same customers you do, but does not compete directly with you, and encourage your customers to visit that business. This can be accomplished through signage, coupons, referrals, and joint advertising. Build a network of businesses that are willing to do the same thing in return and the number of potential customers exposed to your company name will increase with very little expense.

Example: A financial planner had the challenge of competing with several other companies with nationwide name recognition. Regardless of how much advertising money he spent, it was impossible for him to gain the same level of instant identity. One afternoon while waiting for his car to be detailed he started thinking about the places in town his target customers would frequent. As he waited he saw several luxury cars and family minivans come through the auto detail business. Realizing that the owners of these vehicles were the exact clients he was trying to appeal to, he found a non-compete match. Several days later he met with the owner of the detailing shop and requested the opportunity to put his promotional materials on display in the waiting area. They quickly developed several other unique marketing ideas that took advantage of cross promotion.

IN WHAT MANNER HAVE YOU INVITED PEOPLE TO CHOOSE YOU?

It is surprising how simple this concept is, yet how few business owners actually ask for the business. Maybe owners do not have the confidence to ask or haven't found the right words to make the request. Maybe the owner is worried that asking for the business makes them look desperate for business. However, a simple question phrased in a professional way, delivered at the right time, can make the difference between a patron and a passerby.

Example: Years ago we had our house painted and were very pleased with the result. When five years had passed we received a card from the painter in the mail. He enclosed a simple newsletter that updated us on his business growth and added a hand-written personal note that asked us to keep him in mind when we were ready to repaint our house. He followed up the card with a phone call. When we decided it was time to repaint, his business was the first we considered. A good job, followed by a timely card and a simple phone call, proved to be a very cost-effective invitation for this business.

CAN YOU PACKAGE YOUR SERVICE DIFFERENTLY TO MAKE IT MORE ATTRACTIVE?

Learning how to package things together, name products differently or create a unique experience is so important to encouraging customers to buy larger quantities of your products. Don't make the mistake of placing your products on shelves to fend for themselves. Help them jump off the rack and into the buyer's hand through attractive packaging and naming.

Example of packaging: Recently I attended a Tupperware party given at a friend's house. I'm sure I have enough plastic containers but admittedly I cannot resist viewing more just for fun. We touched and passed all the new items and commented how handy each piece would be in our collections. Then the hostess used a fantastic selling tool. She promoted a "surprise bag" for the month. For only $29.95 a customer could order a grab bag containing a variety of different handy containers with a guaranteed value well over the investment price. Many attendees ordered it just for the fun of seeing what they would get. While I had intended to buy nothing, I ended up making a significant purchase that evening and it all started with the creative surprise bag. This is a great example of packaging things together differently so as to encourage a buyer.

Example of naming: Spas and salons often make a mistake in naming their services. It does not sound appealing to pay $95 to be wrapped in mud, packed in seaweed or have a deep tissue rub! While making a presentation to a group of massage business owners I challenged them to group the individual services together differently and come up with a more attractive name for the treatments. One attendee caught on to the assignment quickly, deciding that since her therapy room is decorated with stars and moons, she could play off of that theme. Her excitement emerged as a creative idea began to grow from this concept. She decided to combine three of her services, toss in a free relaxation CD and call it "The Celestial Moment". What a dramatic difference that simple change made in the perception of the treatment.

HOW IS YOUR BUSINESS UNIQUE AND EASY TO REMEMBER?

Being different or memorable may be the key to survival. Even if you are selling a product or service that is easily found, be creative and find ways to differentiate your business in the marketplace.

Example: Did the title of my chapter grab your attention? It is the name of my most popular sales and marketing program. Over ten years ago when creating the core content it was given a straightforward name – "Superior Customer Service". Rarely did a client choose it. One day a colleague asked me, "What is the program about?" I replied, " I teach people about the hot ideas for attracting new customers." She said, "Well that reminds me of my favorite Mexican dish. Most of the time when I order it in a restaurant the jalapenos are mixed up in the meat sauce. However, at my favorite restaurant they do it differently. They put the meat in the shell first, add all the toppings and then place the jalapenos across the top in a line. I like it much better that way." I did not understand what any of this had to do with my dilemma. She laughed and said, "I like it that way because I want to see the jalapeno coming. I want to know that the next bite is a hot one. I don't want to look for it. I think your potential clients feel the same way. They want you to show them good ideas for their business, they don't want to look for them!"

For the rest of the day I thought about that phrase – I want to see the jalapeno coming. It was catchy. Maybe used as a new title, it may make the program sound more intriguing. The next day a large organization called to see what programs we had available. Deciding to use this opportunity as a test, I pitched the new title. The meeting planner was so excited because she was creating an entire "south of the border" theme for the meeting. She invited me to present the keynote for the conference knowing little more than my title. Over the next several years the theme has been expanded to include many special touches, which are quite memorable to the attendees. One example is the chile pepper necklaces given out at each seminar. Even though it is a small trinket, the audiences enjoy the token gift, upbeat salsa music and fun foods waiting for them upon arrival. Recently I was at a trade show promoting my business when a woman stopped at my booth and said, "I remember you! You are the jalapeno lady. I have your necklace on my shelf at work and I look at it every day. We have been thinking about hiring you for some training." She didn't remember my name but she remembered my branding. What can you do that makes people think of you first when they have a need for your service?

P.S. ARE YOU BROWSING THIS CHAPTER?

Did you skip to the end of the chapter hoping to get the best "hot tip" in the summary? In order to not disappoint you, here is the most important thing you can do to attract and keep more customers regardless of your product or service.

Many times business owners do everything in their power to make sure that a customer's first experience is a golden moment. Employees are trained to be friendly, the product is great, the experience is worth talking about and the customer is happy to refer others. However, after enough repeat visits, the business begins to feel they have the customer "for life." I see this happen frequently in health care where doctors begin to feel they have branded their patient. "That's my patient" is a common phrase. We must remember that EVERY TIME a person interacts with our company it is a fork in the road. Every time they choose us it is an opportunity to serve them well or fail and run the risk of losing them to the competition. Regardless of how many times they have had a great experience it is today's encounter that counts.

Superior customer service is simple in principle yet difficult to practice. Believe it or not it reminds me of dieting. We all know that burning more calories than what is consumed will lead to weight loss. However, knowing and doing are two different things. Same with my jalapeno recipe. The concept couldn't be much more simplistic yet a majority of people do not do it.

Remember:

- Stay focused on what you are selling.

- Know exactly who your best customers are and have a detailed plan on how to get their attention.

- Be smart about how to create name awareness.

- Create a unique experience for the customer.

- Deliver exceptional service during every encounter.

To receive your free business analysis report, e-mail the author at lguest@laurietalk.com and request the jalapeno report card.

NOTES:

_____
_____
_____
_____
_____
_____
_____
_____
_____
_____
_____
_____
_____
_____
_____
_____
_____
_____
_____
_____
_____
_____
_____
_____
_____
_____
_____
_____

CHAPTER FIVE

Tapping Into Your Teams' Power Traits

How to create a more effective team.

Cindy Kubica

In our ever-changing world, it's no longer about long-term employment—it's about employability. What will make you stand out from other qualified individuals? — Your people skills. Success lies in knowing how to interact well with others.

Life skills expert, Cindy Kubica, has motivated thousands of people to a higher standard of excellence by teaching them how to communicate more effectively, work in a team environment, enhance leadership skills, develop powerful presentation skills, manage stress, and discover a balance between work and personal life.

From shy child to award winning speaker, author, and entrepreneur, Cindy reveals the keys to taking your career to the next level.

Cindy's strategies include:
- Skills to communicate with tact when under pressure
- 5 key elements in creating a dynamic team environment
- Tools and techniques to deal with difficult people
- Eliminating power-robbing speech patterns
- Effective ways to take control from the inside-out
- How to speak up and get your point across

Studio 10 Productions
Franklin, TN • 888-KUBICA4 • www.kubicaspeaks.com

Cindy Kubica

Tapping Into Your Teams' Power Traits

How to create a more effective team.

"What were we thinking?"

After a bad business venture nearly wiped me out financially, I went back to teaching at a local modeling school until I could decide what to do next. It was there that I met photographer Farris Poole, or as he likes to introduce himself, Farris L. Poole, Esquire.

Although Farris is a thin, five feet-seven inches tall, he stands out in a crowd. His unique sense of style makes him easily recognized as an "artsy-fartsy" kind of guy. He has a 1940's feel in his manner of dress, complete with suspenders and a pocket watch. But his trademark is his Fedora, a hat like the one worn by Indiana Jones.

Even though we had just met, it felt as if we had always known each other. We were instant "best friends." It didn't take long for us to realize we also worked well together. I had worked with many photographers over the years, but our special bond made us a great creative team. Farris was the photographer and I was the stylist. As the stylist, I did everything from hair and make-up to dressing and posing the models.

Two years after we met we decided to go into business together and opened a commercial photography studio that includes everything from catalogs to products, CD covers to headshots, and interiors to events. As part of our business, I continued coaching and training people in the entertainment field.

We found the perfect building for our new business venture located on the outskirts of downtown Nashville. It was 2,800 square feet and had a 14-foot ceiling—perfect for commercial photography—plus enough space for a training room. The address was 1013 3rd Avenue, so we decided to drop the 13 and call our business Studio 10.

I didn't have a lot of money to bring to the table—well, $250 to be exact. And Farris, having gone through his own financial challenges, didn't have much money either. In fact, he only had $250 as well. We pooled our money together and paid the first half month's rent. The first night in our new studio, we sat up all night brainstorming about how we were going to make the second half of the rent. As I said, "What were we thinking?"

We rented that building for ten years. In March of 2003, Farris and I bought our own building. Yes, we built a successful business, but less than two years after opening the studio we almost went our separate ways—not due to lack of business, but because of personality conflicts.

Being part of a team, whether it is professional or personal, can be challenging. Eighty-five percent of the success of a team, large or small, is dependent upon how well the team's members interact with each other. There are many facets to an effective team, but your greatest chance for success is to understand what motivates the team members individually and tap into their strengths, or, as I like to call them, 'Power Traits'.

If you don't understand the team members' Power Traits you may inadvertently tap into their weaknesses, which sets them up for possible failure, and sets you up for frustration and disappointment. If your team members have strong personality differences or if they are too much alike—which was the case with Farris and myself—then your team will lack a diversity of strengths.

Have you ever taken a personality test such as Meyers-Briggs, MMPI, David Keirsey's Temperament Sorter, or the SELF test from National Press Publication? If so, then you understand that there are four personality temperaments, each with inherent strengths and weaknesses.

Our temperament is something we are born with—it's who we are naturally. Do you have children, or do you have siblings? Are your children all alike, or are you just like your siblings? Probably not. We are all born with different personalities and our baseline qualities fit into one of the four temperaments.

During my research, I discovered each of the temperaments had an over-all strength and I decided to name them accordingly. They are:

- The Creatives
- The Caretakers
- The Doers
- The Detailers

The Creatives and The Caretakers are right-brain dominant. The right hemisphere is the creative, emotional, and intuitive side of the brain. So-called "right-brained" people are people oriented and view the world in shades of gray.

The Doers and The Detailers are left-brain dominant. The left hemisphere is the linear and logical side of the brain, and controls memory and language functions. So-called "left-brained" people are paper oriented and view the world mostly in black and white.

Right-brained people are generally optimists, while the left-brained people are more often pessimists. Optimists see the bright side of things, while pessimists stress the negative. Most pessimists view themselves as realists.

There are both positive and negative aspects of both types of personalities. When pessimists see a dark alley they think, "Uh-oh, I'd better get out of here. There's probably someone waiting to mug me." When optimists see a dark alley they think, "Ooh, a shortcut."

Regardless of whether a person is an optimist or a pessimist, conflict among the four temperaments is common because they are each motivated in different ways.

As you go through the personality temperaments below, you will recognize the people around you—as well as yourself. In addition to your primary temperament, you will probably find that you have some of the traits of a secondary temperament.

THE CREATIVES

The Creatives are natural leaders and are motivated by fast-paced, short-term assignments where they are free to use their creativity. They work best when their job is ever changing and even enjoy a degree of risk. They are hard working, confident, direct, and open. Because they are social by nature, they work well with people.

They are charismatic and can easily motivate others to try new ideas and new ways of doing things. The Creatives thrive on attention and are highly motivated by public accolades.

The Creatives' offices are usually a mess, but they know where everything is. They will go through phases where they try to get organized. One week they'll use the Paper Tiger filing system, become bored with it, and change to color-coding.

In a nutshell, The Creatives' Power Traits:

- Charismatic
- Persuasive
- Risk takers
- Thrive on change
- Inspiring
- Natural leaders

- Confident
- Open & Direct
- Competitive
- Socially skilled
- Fast thinkers
- Like attention

THE CARETAKERS

The Caretakers are motivated by feeling needed and enjoy taking care of others. They will quickly volunteer to help with whatever needs to be done, are enthusiastic, and are real team players. They affirm others and are devoted. They are intuitive and can quickly and easily identify what others want and need. When there is discord they will rush in to play the part of the peacemaker and negotiator. The Caretakers are also social by nature and are trusting.

The Caretakers typically have a candy dish on their desks, and their offices glisten with personal effects. They decorate for holidays and remember everyone's birthday.

In a nutshell, The Caretakers' Power Traits:

- Team players
- Caring
- Enthusiastic
- Accessible
- Sensitive
- Affirm others
- Social

- Peacemakers
- Devoted
- Accommodating
- Trusting
- Good listeners
- Intuitive

THE DOERS

The Does are natural leaders and are motivated by accomplishment. If you give them a list of 20 tasks they will stick to the list until every item is checked off. They are ambitious, organized, and dependable. They have their systems for doing things, and as long as those systems are working, they are not likely to change. The Doers are very direct and will quickly speak up if something is not being done to their satisfaction.

The Doers' offices are generally neat, and void of personal items such as photos and memorabilia. They are more likely to display plaques and trophies from accomplishments.

In a nutshell, The Doers' Power Traits:

- Ambitious
- Organized
- Very direct
- Systematic
- Practical
- Goal-oriented
- Dependable
- Self-determined
- Traditional
- Natural Leaders

THE DETAILERS

The Detailers are logical and happiest when they have all the facts. They are meticulous, taking their time to be sure they have well-thought-out, detailed plans. The Detailers have high standards and, like the Doers, have their systems for doing things. Unlike the Doers, they are reserved, mild mannered, and avoid conflict. They also prefer working alone. The Detailers are quiet by nature but often surprise others with their dry wit.

The Detailers like having their offices neat and orderly, though they are not always able to keep them that way. They get caught up in the details of whatever they are focused on, and an orderly office becomes secondary.

In a nutshell, The Detailers Power Traits:

- Logical
- Factual
- Have high values
- Calm
- Consistent in their style
- Well-thought-out, detailed plans
- Thorough
- Reserved
- Avoid conflict
- Mild mannered
- Practical

Do you recognize yourself as one of these temperaments? Do you have strengths from a secondary temperament as well? Do you recognize the members of your team?

CHALLENGES WITH TEMPERAMENTS

Along with its strengths, each of the four temperaments has its own set of challenges. The very things that make people valuable as team members can also be points of conflict. In other words, their blessing is their curse and their curse is their blessing.

The Creatives

The challenge in working with The Creatives is that they get bored easily and have a difficult time with follow-through. They procrastinate, putting things off until the last moment so they can get that adrenaline rush that helps them focus. The Creatives are less likely to create a plan of action; they prefer making it up as they go along. They are not known for their punctuality, and because they are social by nature, they are easily distracted by chitchat. If you put a group of Creatives together, they will likely go to lunch.

The Caretakers

The challenge when working with The Caretakers is that they tend to over-commit. They have a hard time saying "no" and end up becoming overwhelmed. They have a strong need to be liked or loved, and when they are not, they will work hard to win others over. Put a group of Caretakers together they will all be trying to wait on each other.

The Doers

Because The Doers are task oriented, they don't want to hear excuses and have no time for idle chitchat. Their lack of people skills often makes them hard to work with, which causes others to stay at arm's length. They are Type A personalities and are hard on themselves when they don't meet or exceed their own expectations. If you put a group of Doers together, they will argue about whose way is the right way to get the job done.

The Detailers

The Detailers are often viewed as slow because they won't act or make a decision until they have all the facts, and are certain that all the facts are correct. It can be frustrating for The Doers and The Creatives who prefer to work quickly. The Detailers often work so hard at avoiding conflict, that they actually cause it. Put a group of Detailers together, and they will go off into their own corners and begin gathering facts.

How different—or even how alike—you are with a member of your team can be a source of conflict (for more on conflict, read Toni Boyles' chapter). The problem Farris and I had was that in many ways we were too much alike. We are both Creatives. Neither of us likes paperwork, and we each have a hard time with follow-through on long-term projects.

When we started our business, Farris tried to lean on me for the detail work and it would frustrate both of us. I hated it as much as he did but of the two of us, I was the one who was better at the "business" end of our business.

Farris is highly creative, easily excitable, and dramatic. He is also near genius. He seems to know something about any topic you can bring up and his memory for facts and details is amazing. But when it comes to handling the "business" end of our business, to say that he has shortcomings would be an understatement—particularly when it comes to money. I can give him one check to deposit and he will add it up wrong!

He knows I say this about him, and one afternoon, he called me and said, "I hate it when you're right."

I said, "What did you do, Farris?"

He said, "You know that $300 check you gave me to deposit, and you said to keep $50 out for petty cash? Well I have $250 in my hand."

Is it frustrating? Very! But whether he's good with finances is not what makes us money. His creative mind and eye for detail make him an exceptional photographer. That's what makes us money, and that's what I choose to stay focused on—his Power Traits.

As I began my study on personality types and temperaments I realized what was wrong with our business: we needed a Detailer. We needed someone whose power traits included the ability to follow through on the paperwork, bookkeeping, and most of all someone who would file our sales taxes in a timely fashion.

Once we added The Detailer, Gary, to our team the success of our company soared. Does Gary get frustrated with Farris and me? Sure! He prefers a detailed plan of action, and Farris and I like to make it up as we go along. For us, when we spend too much time on details it kills our creativity. No creativity, no business. No control over the day-to-day business, no business.

In 1995 Farris and I decided to expand the educational side of our business. I moved from coaching and training entertainers to speaking and training for corporate America and related associations. With Farris' intellect and Gary's eye for detail, they have helped me create dynamic and informative programs, books, and audio series. Once again, through drawing on the Power Traits of my team, that side of our business has become wonderfully successful as well.

There are many challenges in working with a team; the biggest is in dealing with all the different personalities.

The success of your team lies within the natural strengths of its members. Identify what those strengths are, along with any weaknesses. Coach them to straighten their weaknesses, but stay focused on using each member's Power Traits. Success awaits you.

CHAPTER SIX

Connecting With Success

Strategies for building your personal network.

Nancy J. Lewis, MS, PHR

Nancy J. Lewis is a leading motivational/inspirational keynote speaker, trainer, author, and human resources consultant. She is the president of Progressive Techniques, Inc. based in Fayetteville, Georgia where the theme of her organization is "Developing a Better YOU!" She has been speaking and conducting training for 20 years. She earned a M.S. degree from Georgia State University in Urban and Public Affairs with a concentration in Human Resources. Nancy works with organizations that want to grow their people and with people who want more impact in their lives and careers. She conducts dynamic keynotes and seminars on customer service, leadership, diversity, human resources, and personal enrichment. Nancy delivers customized, energizing, interactive, and content-rich presentations that provide strategies for everyday living.

Nancy is the co-author of *Sisters Together: Lessons Learned That Have Anchored Our Souls* and author of *Things To Do To Be A Better YOU!*

Nancy is a member of National Speakers Association (NSA) and many other professional organizations. She is called the "Speaker With A Presence."

Progressive Techniques, Inc.
Fayetteville, GA • 800-445-9385 • www.nancyjlewis.com

Nancy J. Lewis, MS, PHR

Connecting With Success

Strategies for building your personal network.

The term "networking" is used frequently from the boardroom to the social room. Savvy networking has become a very necessary skill for advancing your career and making business contacts. It is not about who you know, but rather who knows you and what they know about you.

In *Power Networking, 55 Secrets for Personal & Professional Success,* Donna Fisher and Sandy Vilas share the following information. Did you know that:

- A referral generates 80% more results than a cold call.

- Approximately 70% of all jobs are found through networking.

- Most people you meet have at least 250 contacts.

- Anyone you might want to meet or contact is only four to five people away from you.

Vast resources are available to you to help you achieve what you desire in life. Fisher and Vilas state that the secrets to success lie not in what you do but in how you do it and how well you network with others along the way.

The *American Heritage College Dictionary* defines "networking" in the following way: An informal system whereby persons having common interests assist each other. Networking requires people skills we constantly cultivate and develop throughout our lifetime.

Anyone can network at anytime anywhere; it is the equivalent of nonstop networking. The skill of connecting with others is a powerful, invaluable technique for building mutually beneficial contacts.

Networking affords us the opportunity to nurture our professional, personal, and social contacts by obtaining 1) information, 2) support, and 3) referrals in a spirit of sharing that goes beyond information or ideas. Effective networkers demonstrate this spirit by constantly sharing with others. They recognize that building relationships takes time and does not happen overnight. They understand the value of marketing their own product or service.

Some individuals feel networking is a game and they must learn the rules to play. Networking is much more than a game. We are in an era where people do business, solidify deals, and advance careers on relationships they have developed over time. It is key you learn to master the art of working a room and effectively networking in the process. Whether you are corporately attached or an entrepreneur, this skill is critical to your success. Smart networking is building relationships that are mutually supportive and empowering. It is about success, accomplishments, and having the confidence to work with others to get a favorable outcome.

STRATEGIES FOR NETWORKING:

#1: Define Your Support System

The first strategy of networking is defining your support system. Stop and think, about who the people are in your network and those you interact with on a regular basis.

- Family members
- Neighbors
- Family doctor/dentist
- Friends
- Family mechanic

- Hairstylist
- Business colleagues
- Family minister
- Spouse/significant other
- Parents of your children's friends

All of the people listed above know people you can have access to because of your mutual connection. Take time to sit down and list the names of the people that you can use as a reference. Look at those that are closely aligned with you, your core network group and those with whom you interact less frequently. As you create this list, categorize in the area of personal affiliations, organizational/community affiliations, professional affiliations, and others. The key thing is to take action and make the list.

Personal affiliations are those persons who know you on a one-on-one basis. Our network of family and friends fall in this area. We often discount this group when we start to network. Community/organizational affiliations are organizations you are involved in that may or may not be career related. It may be volunteering at your church, synagogue, board of directors, foundations, political activities, fraternities/sororities, PTA, etc. Getting active on a committee creates involvement and a connection, which is simply networking. Professional affiliations are those connections that lead to career advantages. Some of the professional contacts are co-workers, vendors, clients, and competitors. No matter what your goal and role in life, your ability to cultivate a strong, stable, and supportive network system is critical to your success. The other category is those unexpected meetings that take place in the grocery store, on the airplane, on the subway, and in the parking lot. These are opportunities that have the potential for changing your life.

Strategy #2: Know Yourself

The second strategy for networking success is to know yourself. You must be keenly aware of your own needs and goals. Networking pro Alice Ostrower insists self-awareness is the key to effective networking. She says, "Each person has to be comfortable with him/herself first." You must be able to communicate clearly what you need before others can help you. It is important to know your personal strengths and career goals. By knowing these, it makes you more effective at sharing your experiences and desires in networking situations.

Strategy #3: Understand The Rules for How to Work a Room

The third strategy for networking success is understanding the rules for how to work a room. I have found the following strategies helpful when networking in social settings.

1. Determine what you are going to do first, eat or network.

2. If you attend a lot of networking events, invest in a nice name badge.

3. Wear your name badge on your right side. This is because most people shake with their right hand and as they do, they will have a direct line of sight to your name.

4. Engage in dialogue for 3-5 minutes before exchanging business cards. This gives you the opportunity to exchange information and make a connection with the person you are talking to.

5. Use conversation energizers (basic questions to initiate dialogue) when meeting people. (For example, How did you find out about this event?)

6. When exchanging cards, make sure you look at the card and take note of the person's name before you put it away. This shows the person you appreciate receiving the card.

7. Stay focused on the person you are talking to; don't have roaming eyes. Positive eye contact says, "I want to interact with you."

8. Make notes on the card to help jog your memory about the person and your discussion.

9. Smile and greet people with a firm handshake. Remember everyone is not a hugger. Carry your drink in your left hand, leaving your right hand free to greet new people.

10. When ending a conversation, be polite and courteous. Remind those you are talking to you had a goal to meet a certain number of people and you must continue to circulate to achieve that goal.

11. Make sure your business cards are accessible and take more business cards than you will need to the event.

Strategy #4: The Three R's of Networking

The fourth strategy for networking success is The Three R's of Networking. The first "R" stands for being real. How do you demonstrate that? Simply be who you are all the time; put away the facades and be genuine. Learn how to be true to yourself no matter who you are talking to. Don't try to be what you feel others expect you to be. It won't work and you will come across as pompous, phony, and insincere, which is the kiss of death in networking. Recognize that real also stands for "Respecting Everyone's Authenticity in Life." Using this approach, there is no hidden agenda about what you want or who you are because the secrets to success lie not in what you do, but in how you do it.

The second "R" stands for establishing rapport. How do you go about developing rapport? Establishing rapport means building strong lines of communication. This requires greeting those you meet with a smile while making introductions. You must have an attitude of receptivity and an interest in the persons with whom you are talking. Make sure you listen carefully, repeat their name and use it in the conversation. This adds the personal touch. As always, use the name with moderation.

The third "R" stands for relationships. The goal of successful networking is to build relationships so that the exchange of ideas, information, resources, and opportunities can occur. It is important to build relationships that are mutually supportive. Building relationships ensures success, accomplishment, and confidence in working with others. It also facilitates connecting people for results. You must generate interest and responsiveness in maintaining your relationships. As you give more than you receive, watch how you are blessed with more than you need. Constantly approach people and ask what they are doing and how you can support them. Remember you must continue to cultivate relationships. Let's consider the concept of a fishing net. It takes all the knots to make the fishing net work.

Strategy #5: Understanding the Four Reasons for Networking

The fifth strategy for successful networking is understanding the four reasons for networking.

1. The first is information. We all have a vast amount of information that we have collected through our experiences. This information is as unique as we are. Just as you have a wealth of knowledge, so do others that you meet. Strive to be an expert on a topic; to set yourself apart from everyone else. Remember as I mentioned earlier in the chapter, 70% of jobs are filled through networking. The majority of my business has been attributed to the power of networking.

2. The second reason for networking is influence. George Fraser, author of *Success Runs in Our Race,* states that he translates influence to mean access to key people. Fraser goes on saying that the next best thing to knowing someone with the power is knowing someone who knows that person. Think of our fishing net again. The knots symbolize the relationship between two different people with mutual interests. The knots link them together. It is important to know those persons who are able to link you up with persons who can assist you in achieving your goals. Think of all the opportunities you have to connect with persons who can provide valuable insight to your success through work, volunteering, church, and all your activities.

3. The third reason for networking is resources. At different stages of your career, you will need some of the following resources: advertising, marketing, products, or services. This is where human resources are important, especially if you work in organizations where there is limited funding. It is vital to know where to go to get the resources to move the projects further.

4. The fourth reason for networking is for personal reasons. I find it very rewarding to be involved in different organizations. The challenge is not to overextend yourself and learn how to say no. It is not just a matter of involvement but being committed to the organization, seeking to meet and know people who have similar motives, but with different backgrounds and skill sets. As we come together for the common goal, we learn to share and identify strengths to enhance our resources.

Strategy #6: Networking OOPS!

The sixth strategy for successful networking is avoid Networking OOPS! Be mindful of some of the following OOPS!

1. Don't interrupt a conversation in progress. Wait until there is a break in the conversation to get involved.

2. Don't be unapproachable.

3. Don't update your business cards on site. (In other words, avoid striking through and changing your phone number, email, etc. on location.)

4. Never use profanity.

5. Don't monopolize the conversation.

6. Never have more to drink than you can handle.

Strategy #7: Follow up

The seventh strategy for successful networking is follow up. Once you have developed the skill, it becomes imperative that you follow up with phone calls, note cards, breakfast/luncheon meetings, or whatever is necessary to develop the relationship. When you meet new people that you have connected with, try and contact them within 48-72 hours via an email, personal note card, or by phone. Start a tickler file for notes about when you need to follow up. It has been through this system that I have created opportunities and you can do the same thing. Your ability to network depends on your willingness to step out of your comfort zone. Once you step out of your comfort zone, boundaries disappear.

SUMMARY

In summary, the seven strategies for successful networking are:

1. Develop a strong support system

2. Know yourself

3. Understand the guidelines for how to work a room

4. Develop the Three R's of networking

5. Identify and understand the four reasons for networking

6. Identify and understand Networking OOPS!

7. FOLLOW UP, FOLLOW UP, FOLLOW UP

Several years ago I was speaking at a conference in New Orleans and met a very influential business executive. We began to talk and exchange information about our businesses. When we parted, he said to keep in touch. After many voice mails, emails, and follow up, he was instrumental in helping me secure two big clients. The moral of the story is it takes time to build relationships and formulate alliances, but if you become diligent in the rules of networking you will have success. The choice is yours. HAPPY NETWORKING!

CHAPTER SEVEN

Don't Go Hunting Bears With a Stick

Understanding gender differences in the workplace.

Ann E. Mah

Ann Mah, owner of Discover!Strategies, works with women's organizations across the nation on strategies for life and business. Her thought-provoking and practical approach to learning and leading sends participants home with ideas they can use immediately. Topics most requested are managing change, men and women at work, presentation skills, business etiquette, networking, and developing a winning personal style.

A past national president of the American Business Women's Association, Ann knows the issues that matter most to women. She brings the teaching style of a seasoned educator and over 20 years of experience in corporate management to her seminars. Ann connects to her audience through personal stories and a fun approach to learning. She provides customized workshops and keynotes for companies and conventions.

Ann is the business skills writer for HersKansas magazine and holds a masters degree in education. Workshops available include:

- Don't Go Hunting Bears With a Stick
- Managing the Challenge of Change
- Making Waves – Developing Your Own Personal Style
- Oh Behave! Business Etiquette Essentials
- Skills That Pay the Bills

Ann E. Mah
Topeka, KS • 785-266-9434 • www.annmah.com

Ann E. Mah

Don't Go Hunting Bears With a Stick

Understanding gender differences in the workplace.

Have you ever had the feeling that the men you work with know something you don't know? Well, guess what? They do! Men think, lead and communicate differently from women. The good news is that you also know a few things they don't know; and corporate America needs both styles in the workforce.

Men have been watching each other's backs since the cave days. If women are going to join the hunt, we need to know the "weapons" we come by naturally that will serve us well. We also need to learn about the weapons men have that we can develop. You don't want to go hunting bears with just a stick.

Your natural talents are what I call "standard features". These are talents you were either born with or learned growing up. In addition to these standard features, "options" are available. This chapter will help you recognize your natural talents and how they can work to your advantage. You will also learn about some talents men have that can give you an edge in the workplace.

I learned these lessons the hard way. My wakeup call came when a male co-worker took a juicy assignment I thought should have been mine. In football talk, he clipped me. I fought back "like a girl". I called him names. I talked about him behind his back. I had been betrayed, so I felt he deserved it!

What I came to understand was that in sports and business, clipping is an accepted strategy – especially if it prevents the other team from making a touchdown or sets your team up for the win. Men are rewarded for this kind of behavior – as was my co-worker. If you get clipped, the smart thing to do is get up, wipe off the dirt, get back into the game…and let yesterday's fouls be bygones. It is a talent I needed to learn - an option I needed to develop. I am smarter today and I want you to work smarter, too.

To start, think about the natural talents you bring to the hunt. Women also have unique styles of thinking, leading, and communicating. Recognizing and using these talents makes you more valuable to your company. Think about your own work style. What are some characteristics you have because you are female that work to your advantage in business? What are some characteristics you have because you are female that work against you in business? Make a list of those here:

Characteristics that work for me:

_____

Characteristics that work against me:

_____

We will come back to these later when you make an action plan for improving your business skills.

THINKING IT THROUGH

One of the most glaring natural differences between men and women is how we process information and solve problems. You may already be aware that there are physical differences between male and female brains. In short, the brain is divided into two halves. The left side controls language and speech related skills and the right side controls movement, emotion, and our visual/spatial processing. The two sides are linked through a bundle of nerves called the corpus callosum.

This bundle of nerves is the conduit through which the two halves of the brain communicate. On average, men have a thinner corpus callosum than women. This may explain why men usually attack problems in a linear way and women in a more holistic way. It has also been described as sequential thinking versus conceptual thinking and may help explain why men excel in mathematics and women in the arts.

Another way to think about it is that a man's corpus callosum is like a two-lane road. Information goes in on one lane and out on the other. Men tend to solve problems with one side of the brain. They think sequentially. That is good. A woman's corpus callosum is like a four-lane highway. We can literally carry on several streams of thought at one time and solve problems with both sides of the brain. We think conceptually. That, too, is good.

It translates to the workplace this way. First, if you are making a presentation to a group that is largely men, do it sequentially. Put your points in order - one, two, three. Handle your conversations the same way.

My female boss and I would talk about several things at once. We probably did not even know we were doing it. We talked about work issues, her parents, my son, and a negotiations strategy, all at the same time. When I talk with men one-on-one, I ask one question at a time. I wait for an answer. I have tried to have those multiple-topic conversations with men, and they do not work. They think we cannot stay on track. We appear to be not focused.

I recall a time during contract negotiations when I was on a team with two men. The other side also had one woman and two men. We had a contract five inches thick to review for disputed language. The women wanted to go through the contract and look for identical passages that we already knew appeared in several sections. That would cause us to jump around going through the contract, but would ensure we had consistent language. The men insisted that we start at the beginning and go through each section in order. That way we would be sure to find all the disputed language. Who was right? We all were. We needed to look at the contract both end-to-end and from the "big picture" angle.

The point here is that neither style of thinking and problem solving is good or bad. Further, these characteristics are not absolutes. We certainly have women who are good mathematicians and men who think conceptually. These are simply tendencies we are born with that impact how we relate to each other. You can learn to appreciate the differences, understand them, and use them to your advantage in the hunt.

LEADING FROM THE CENTER

Another valuable talent women learn growing up is the ability to lead from the center. Women tend to put themselves at the center of their organizations rather than at the top. This has been called a "share the power, share the glory" or collaborative approach.

Where did women learn to lead this way? We had lots of practice. Dr. Pat Heim, in her book *Hardball for Women*, explains that girls grow up in a female culture where we learn that everyone wins when we share and compromise. For the most part, we play "one-on-one", usually with a best friend. When girls play games like dolls and house, Heim says, we share power. The purpose of our games is to develop relationships. Success is achieved when we all get along.

Heim notes that competition and conflict are damaging to relationships, so we avoid them. There is no "winning" at dolls. Decisions are made by group consensus and conflicts resolved by compromise. As a result, Heim says, "we learned how to develop and sustain relationships."

What this means for women at work is that our style of leadership drives the level of decision making down into all levels of the organization. The upside is that employees feel empowered. The downside is that there are times when a more direct style of leadership is needed and collaboration put aside.

Here is a case in point. I was an adult counselor for a group of junior high students at a summer camp designed to teach team building. The students were given outdoor activities where they had to work together to solve problems. One time we had just five minutes left to solve a problem. It was clear someone needed to take charge. At that point, the facilitator said that for the remaining time, the boys had to be silent and a girl had to lead. Up to this point the boys had been doing all the talking.

One brave girl stepped forward. Andrea said, "Let's hear everyone's ideas." The boys were livid. There was no time for group consensus. The boys wanted Andrea to step up and tell them what to do, but she did not want to be seen as "bossy". We failed to solve the problem.

After the exercise, I told Andrea that she needed to be aware when to use her natural collaborative style and when to simply step up and give directions. I told her that in this case, the boys viewed her asking their opinion as a sign of weakness; and that sometimes it is okay just to tell people what to do.

The same applies at work. Both collaborative and direct styles are required, and you can learn when to use them. When there is time to fully work through a problem, collaboration is the best style to use. When time is short and decisions must be made quickly, step up and make the call. Given a choice, take respect over being liked when leading men.

Another valuable characteristic we can learn from men is how to work with all the hunters. Because we value relationships so much, women can have difficulty working with people we do not like. We let our personal feelings interfere with our ability to get the job done. Men learn early on that everyone brings some talent to the table. Learn to look past your personal differences and seek out the talents others have that you can use to reach your goals.

If you want a real test of your ability to work with anyone, find someone in your work group with whom you do not get along. Ask that person if there is something you can do to help them on a project. Later on, ask that person to help you out. It could be the beginning of a new networking partnership and a growth experience for both of you. Real leaders use the talents of all the people they have. Learn to be that leader.

CAN YOU HEAR ME NOW?

Men and women approach communication the same way they approach other interactions. In her book *You Just Don't Understand,* Dr. Deborah Tannen explains that men engage in the world through a hierarchical social order in which a person is either one-up or one-down. Women engage in the world through a totally flat hierarchy, trying to give support and reach consensus.

Men's and women's conversations have been described in many ways. Dr. Tannen describes men's conversations as negotiations in which they try to achieve the upper hand. In contrast, women's conversations are an attempt to maintain a connection. Tannen says our styles are a search for independence versus a search for intimacy.

For this reason a man is less likely to appreciate unsolicited advice, as it gives the appearance of being "one down". They are less likely to ask for directions.

Women are more likely to ask for help just to make a connection. Let's take a situation where you are going to the store. A woman would not usually leave home without telling her spouse where she was going. She does this to maintain a connection, even in her absence. He sees it as asking permission, so a man is less likely to tell his spouse he is going to the store.

Again, both styles of conversation are valid. It is just that when we interact, you can see how what you say can be misinterpreted. In the office, the conversation style is likely to be a male style. Be careful that your female style does not leave the impression of incompetence when you are simply doing what women do in conversation.

If you find you are not being heard in meetings, try two things: speak directly and watch your body language. Asking tag questions instead of making direct statements can be a problem for women. Saying, "I feel this plan is the best approach, don't you?" sounds like you are not sure of your position. "Feeling" words also weaken your statements. Say instead, "This plan is the best approach for us". Choose your words to reflect decisiveness and competence.

Body language is also an important part of your communication style. Try taking up more space at the table. Women are generally smaller in size anyway, so don't be a shrinking violet. Sit next to the boss – on his right side if possible. That is the "right-hand man" spot. Spread out your papers. Speak up and do not let others interrupt you. Lean back in your chair. The next time you are in a meeting, notice that the men in charge often relax and sit back. It takes up more space, too!

Finally, learn to use humor when working with men. As boys, they learned to tease each other as a way to connect. They did not forget that when they went to work. They might say something like, "Man, did you sleep in that shirt last night?" just to be funny. A woman would never make a joke like that with another woman for any reason! So if you are having trouble "connecting" with a male co-worker, add a little humor to the situation. You can be a great communicator if you learn the language of the other hunters!

USING THE WEAPONS OF GENDER

I hope I have given you a few things to think about and that you will incorporate some of these ideas into your arsenal of career weapons. In fact, you can start right now.

Take a look at the list of characteristics you made at the start of this chapter. Think about an aspect of your leadership, thinking, or communication style that could use some development and write it below.

One talent I need to work on is:

_____

I can develop this talent through:

_____ Reading books/listening to tapes

_____ Getting a mentor

_____ Talking to my boss

_____ Taking a professional development class

ONE MORE HUNTING STORY

I had to laugh at summer camp when on the last morning we were getting ready to leave and once more the students played out their roles perfectly. There were the girls, getting ready together. "Do I look pretty?" Yes, we are all pretty now, so let's go. They wanted to be sure everyone looked their best.

Outside in the yard, the boys were getting ready, too. One of them had a stick and he hit a wasp's nest. Then the rest of the boys ran around screaming, killing wasps with a stick. I guess someone had to be "one-down", and that day it was the wasps. Somehow it was not a far cry from hunting bears.

My wish for you is that you will get what you are looking for out there in the hunt, and that you have all the weapons you need!

NOTES:

_____

_____

_____

_____

_____

_____

_____

_____

_____

_____

_____

_____

_____

_____

_____

_____

_____

_____

_____

_____

_____

_____

_____

_____

CHAPTER EIGHT

Communicating for Success

How to pull rank when you have no rank to pull.

Sarita Maybin

Sarita Maybin is an award-winning professional speaker who has trained thousands of people in 47 states, Canada, England, Hong Kong, Singapore & Malaysia. Some of her favorite clients include Hewlett Packard, NASA, the National Weather Service, PGA and the Las Vegas Convention Center. Her expertise and previous experience includes a Masters Degree in Counseling and thirteen years as a supervisor in University Administration. She is also a Toastmasters Humorous speech contest winner and a past president of the San Diego Chapter of the National Speakers Association.

Sarita offers customized training solutions designed to help your team work together better. Or, select one of her five most popular seminars & keynote speeches:

- How to Turn Negativity into Possibility…
  At Work and Beyond
- Total Teamwork
- How to Get More Done with Less Stress
- Communicating for Success
- Adapting, Succeeding and Thriving in the Workplace

Sarita Maybin
Oceanside, CA • 800-439-8248 • www.saritatalk.com

<u>Sarita Maybin</u>

Communicating for Success
How to pull rank when you have no rank to pull.

In this chapter you will learn:

- How to gain cooperation and get your ideas heard
- How to receive criticism gracefully…without getting defensive
- The two "green jello" principles for conflict resolution

PULLING RANK

How do you pull rank when you have no rank to pull? That was the question asked of me a few years ago by one of my seminar participants. She wanted to know how to gain cooperation from coworkers, supervisors and others in the organization over whom she had no official authority.

My response was two-fold:

Let them know the "W.I.I.F.M." – That's "What's in it for me?"

People want to know what's in it for them to go along with what you want. Human behaviorists long ago demonstrated that what motivates human beings is the ability to see that a certain course of action will in some way be rewarding. Or, at the very least they want to avoid some awful fate. As they say in my daughter's pre-teen circle of friends: "And I care because?...." The little voice in the heads of some of your co-workers may be uttering those very words. As you make requests of those in your workplace or business community, it would certainly make sense to share with them how their helping you will benefit them.

For example:
- Will co-workers' involvement in your project give them visibility and allow them to connect with people they want to know?

- If your boss approves your workshop attendance, will the department save time and money as a result of the skills you'll learn?

- Will your colleague finally have the opportunity to use a certain area of expertise by participating in your committee?

- Will their cooperation simply allow them the opportunity to win your undying gratitude?

(As I like to say, "I will be eternally grateful if you could help me with...")

Let them have a vote. Make requests, not demands.

In this era of "doing more with less" and never ending deadlines, it's tempting to make demands, dictate orders and even threaten. Anything to get the job done! However, your colleagues will be more appreciative and more likely to cooperate if you communicate your needs using respectful requests rather than ranting and raving. The thing about requests, though, is that the other person gets a "vote". They can choose to say "no".

Fortunately, though, as you've learned from some of the other chapters in this book, building a solid network, developing a professional image and encouraging a team approach can serve as a solid foundation for positive communication. Translation: If people like and respect you they are more likely to want to say "Yes!" to your requests.

On the following page are words and phrases that squash the urge to cooperate AND those that promote and encourage cooperation:

Words and Phrases to AVOID

"You need to"
"You better"
"You have to"
"You will"
"If you don't do this then…"
"You should"
"You know what you should do…"

Words and Phrases to USE

"Would you be willing to"
"Would you consider"
"Would it be possible to"
"Could we try"
"What do you think about"
"What if"
"How about"
"I need your help"
"I would appreciate"
"I need"
"I would like"

RULE #1 FOR RECEIVING CRITICISM

Twenty years ago my graduate school mentor shared with me the best advice I've ever received on communicating for success. She shared with me Rule #1 for gracefully receiving criticism without getting defensive.   Rule # 1: When you receive criticism, ASK FOR MORE. More information, that is.

By the way, this is the only rule. There is no Rule #2, or #3, or…

Some of my favorite phrases for "asking for more" include:

"How do you mean?"
"Can you be more specific"
"Can you give me an example?"
"Could you elaborate please?"
"Tell me more"

And to take it one step further, you can solicit input from the person sharing the criticism by asking for their suggestions.

These phrases include:

"What do you suggest?"
"What would you like to see happen?"
"What do you think we should do?"
"How should we resolve it?"
"In your opinion, what should be done?

One occasion on which I was able to successfully apply this advice vividly stands out in my mind. When I worked in university administration, I would hold a weekly one-on-one meeting with each member of my staff. On one such occasion I had just come back from supervisor training. They had reminded us of the importance of soliciting input from our staff. Staff opinions on ways to improve the department were deemed especially important. Eager to try this out, I launched into this conversation:

Sarita: "Bill, how do you think we could improve our department?"
Bill: "Well, Sarita, I think YOU could be a better supervisor!"

(Long pause as Sarita fights off the urge to get defensive and "write Bill up" for insubordination. Sarita chooses the "ask for more" strategy instead.)

Sarita: "A better supervisor? How do you mean?"
Bill: "It would be helpful if you could give us more specific feedback on how we are doing…. Maybe, at each one-on-one meeting tell us one thing we're doing well and one thing we need to improve. Some of us are not sure how you feel about how well we're doing in our jobs"
Sarita: "I could do that. We'll start with next week's one-on-one meeting!"

Rule #1: "ASK FOR MORE" served me well on that day. (And, it continues to help me receive criticism gracefully…even as I fight the urge to cup my hands over my ears and chant "I don't hear you, I don't hear you…").   I cringe to think how that scenario with my employee might have turned out if I had instead chosen to get defensive. It certainly would have done nothing to further the positive communication process.

"GREEN JELLO" PRINCIPLES OF CONFLICT RESOLUTION

One of the most crucial skills in communicating for success is the ability to effectively resolve conflict. I was reminded of the two most important aspects of conflict resolution one Sunday morning about seven years ago when my daughter was about four years old. Since that day, I refer to the two important aspects of conflict resolution as the "green jello" principles. They are:

Principle #1: Figure out the REAL agenda

Often the real –sometimes "hidden" – agenda in a conflict is something like ego, turf, power, control or other self-serving issues. You may have noticed this both at work and at home.

Principle #2:   Have a plan b (or c, d…)

When you go into a conflict situation, do you just have one idea about how the conflict might be resolved? If so, you may find yourself getting "ugly" and inflexible when the other person chooses not to "buy into" your way of doing things. It's always helpful to have a plan b, c, d….

Anyway…my big epiphany regarding the two principles came on a Sunday morning seven years ago. I was standing in the kitchen fixing breakfast. This is always a big deal because I don't cook a big breakfast every day. Just on Sundays.

My daughter, who was four years old at the time, came into the kitchen, opened the refrigerator and noticed a four-pack of green jello.

"Mommy" she asked "May I have a green jello?"

At this point I hesitated, contemplating whether or not I

wanted to give her a green jello. After all, I was fixing breakfast. However, I say "OK, you may have a green jello.".

She takes the jello, slurps it up and returns only moments later. "May I have another green jello?"

This time I said "No…you may NOT have another green jello".

What do you think happened next?

Whether you have children or not, you can probably guess correctly. She dropped to the floor in a tantrum. She shrieked in a high pitched, shrill, whiny voice that sounded much like the sound of fingernails scratching against a chalkboard. "I want jello, I want jello!"

As my daughter writhed on the floor in a full blown tantrum, I looked at her. Without sympathy, I said "Crying will not help you. You may not have another green jello".

Let's talk now about the husband.

Husband: (shouting from the living room): "Give her the @*# jello!"

Sarita: "Honey, I'd rather not give her the jello. I'm fixing breakfast."

Husband: "What's the BIG DEAL! Just give her the jello!"

Sarita: "I'd rather not"

Do you sense a conflict brewing?

At that point, husband and I are at each other's throats.

"Jello!"

"No Jello!"

"Jello!"

"No Jello!"

"What's wrong with this picture?" I asked myself. "I make a living teaching others conflict resolution, teamwork, dealing with negativity, and communication skills. Surely I was NOT engaged in a conflict over…."GREEN JELLO!!!?"

Then it occurred to me… the two important aspects of conflict. The "green jello principles!

Principle #1: Figure out the REAL AGENDA

So…what might have been husband's "not so hidden" agenda in this Sunday morning scenario?

You guessed it…SHUT THE CHILD UP!

And, what might have been my agenda? When I've shared this story in my presentations I have heard many speculations about my REAL agenda:

"I'm cooking breakfast over this hot stove...somebody better eat!" (Ego)
"Crying will NOT be rewarded!" (Discipline)
"I'm the mommy here!" (Control)
"I want those other jellos for myself!" (Self Serving)
"Shut husband up!" (Power/Turf)

This is no different than how conflict happens outside of the kitchen, in the workplace.

Coworkers may say: "Our department can't support that program because of pressing deadlines for our priority projects!"

Yet, what they may really mean is:

"You didn't help us with our project last year, so we're not going to help YOU!"   (Self serving)

"That project should really be ours!" (Ego, turf)

"If we can't do the project the way we want we don't want to be part of it!" (Control)

So...often it's not really about the "proverbial green jello" after all. Yet, many times we get caught up on the superficial and overlook the real underlying issue. The trick in this type of situation is to ask questions and explore further.

Key phrases for digging beneath the surface to find out what's really going on:

"I'm getting the impression that..."
"I'm sensing that"
"I noticed _____ and I'm wondering _____."
"It seems like..."

Principle #2:   *Have a plan b (or c, d...)*

Especially at work, isn't it interesting that we often bring only one option to the table in a conflict situation? The goal then, is to have as many options in mind as possible AND be open to options that may be proposed by the other person as well. Have you noticed that the most negative and desperate people are those who feel they have no choice? No options? The more choices and options we have the more positive we can be in general, and the more productive in resolving conflicts in particular.

Which brings me back to the kitchen that Sunday morning seven years ago.

Husband's agenda was peace and quiet...and perhaps some need to control the situation.

My agenda ranged from discipline and control to my own self-serving goal of hoarding the jello for myself.

So...the million-dollar question: What plan b, or plan c, will address these agendas? WHAT ARE THE OPTIONS?

Again, those who have heard me tell this story, have shared many thoughts on all the possible options:

"Just let her eat all four jellos"

"Tell her she can have more jello after breakfast"

"Send her to a 'time out' "

"Distract her with something else to do"

"Tell the husband to get her the jello himself"

I contemplated the many options available to me. One of the items on my breakfast menu that day — although not a great testimony to my cooking ability – was the pastry that pops open when you strike the package against the corner of the counter. It is usually accompanied by a plastic container of frosting.

"If you can get up off the floor and act like a big girl", I said to my daughter, "then you can assist me in preparing breakfast. What do you think about being in charge of frosting the pasties?"

(Did you notice? That's the "Distract her with something else" option.)

She leapt up from the floor and happily frosted the pastries. Hmmm...once again, it wasn't even really about the green jello.

Conflict resolved. Peace and quiet for husband. No spoiled appetite and the remaining three jellos are still intact. The next time you find yourself in a conflict — in the kitchen or in the staff meeting – dig beneath the superficial "green jello". Use the key phrases provided above to figure out the real agenda. Explore the options by asking such questions as:

"What are our options"

"How can we resolve this"

"How can we make this work?"

"What do you need from me?"

"Could you live with it if we..."

"How might we gain your cooperation?"

So, the secret to communicating for success lies in being able to elicit the cooperation of colleagues, accepting criticism without getting defensive, and arming yourself with options in conflict situations.

CHAPTER NINE

Step Up and Lead

Leading for Loyalty in the 21st Century.

Susan Meyer-Miller

An international speaker and trainer, Susan Meyer has spoken to a half-million people in 8 countries. She is a business trainer, management consultant, motivational speaker and the author of a book entitled *SOS! 101 Solutions to Overcome Stress*. Her wide range of topics include Stress Management and Leadership Skills

A native Kansan, Susan graduated from the University of Kansas with a BA in Human Resources Management. After a fulfilling career in restaurant management and training, Susan then traveled extensively as a Management Consultant and Trainer for Fred Pryor Seminars where she achieved consistently high customer ratings and trained and mentored many new speakers.

Susan now owns a training company – SpeakerUSA – where she takes pride in customizing training to meet the specific needs of her clients. Susan is an active writer currently publishing two newsletters and has won both regional and national awards for her efforts.

She is also active in her community and was named "Business Associate of the Year" in 1999 and "Woman of the Year" in 2002 from the local American Business Women's Association chapter where she has held many leadership roles.

SpeakerUSA
Shawnee, KS • 877-674-8446 • www.speakerusa.com

Susan Meyer-Miller

Step Up and Lead
Leading for Loyalty in the 21st Century.

Project management, promotion to team leader, or pandemonium—everyone is called upon to step up and lead occasionally. Sometimes you plan for it; sometimes you don't. Sometimes you set a goal and work your way up. And sometimes, you're sitting there minding your own business, and someone says, "Susan, why don't you handle that?" Well, of course you say, "Sure, I can do that," and POOF! You're a leader! Now what?

Many of us are technical experts called upon to take responsibility of supervising a team with little or no training in people management. Others find their job requires leading project teams to solve problems or implement changes with little authority. Some have their sights set on moving into higher leadership positions within the company. Whatever YOUR situation, developing and demonstrating your leadership skills at work will pay off. Leadership has many rewards including seeing others grow and celebrating success as a team. And who knows? You might just raise your income in the process.

Ready or not finding yourself in a leadership role is a great opportunity to let your strengths shine. Step up and lead! Start where you are. Even a seasoned leader knows she is always learning, growing and taking on new challenges. Leaders exude confidence. They help others build confidence— in themselves, in their projects, and in their products. The aim of this chapter is to give you the confidence to step up and lead by outlining some of the skills of the best leaders. Start by making a list of the best managers, coaches or role models you have had; add to that one or two public leaders you admire. Next, think of the specific situations in which you admired them most. What did they do? What did they say? How did they look? What makes a great leader? Read on , and I'll bet some of your answers will match the list below of the most often listed traits of today's successful leaders.

GREAT LEADERS SEE THE FUTURE...

...and they paint a clear picture for us. Great leaders are visionary. They are acutely aware of their surroundings and the dynamic nature of life and business. They watch for trends and imagine how things will be next year or in five years or ten. To make these analysis they read and study both history and the news about their industries. And they study people. Who are their customers? What are they interested in? What do they need? What about their team members? Great leaders are deep thinkers who take the time to envision what the future might be—or could be—in their areas of influence. Then they share it with others.

Many people think they can see the future, yet it takes a leader to really communicate her vision. The great leader can describe in detail where she is headed in a way that will make people want to follow along. How do you communicate your vision?

Here are some effective ways to help others see the future.

- Create a mission statement as a guiding "battle cry" toward the vision.

- Describe in great detail what success looks like or how it might feel to achieve. What do people say?

- Discuss the future in daily conversations with team members.

- Set written goals, manageable objectives and action steps to clearly define what success looks like.

- Recognize and reward members' actions toward making the vision real. Celebrate success!

- Use repetition. Include the vision in interviewing, , training, appraisals, and newsletters. Make the vision so clear each team member can describe it.

GREAT LEADERS DEMONSTRATE OWNERSHIP

"Leaders are People who have decided to make a difference regardless of the circumstances." — *Jim Rohn*

There are many stories in business, sports and the military demonstrating how leaders took ownership for their team and for their results bad or good. The great coach Vincent Lombardi once said, "When the team wins, they get all the credit, but when they lose, it's my fault." He understood the concept of "ownership" and knew that all the excuses in the world would not take away the fact that as the coach, he was accountable for the team's success. He hired them, he coached them, he designed the strategy, he focused them before the game. He also understood the value of giving up the credit when the team won.

Many people today refuse to take ownership for their jobs preferring instead to blame others or make excuses as to why they aren't getting results. "You can't get good help these days," they say, or "The economy is down and people just aren't buying." Some people wonder why they can't get a good raise or have been waiting years for that promotion. Likely, it is because rather than finding ways to solve problems and overcome obstacles, they make excuses, blame or complain. Great leaders emerge because, they take ownership of the situations they find themselves in and take initiative to find ways to reach their targets by overcoming obstacles. Take ownership for your results! Keep your word. And when you do find a legitimate obstacle in your path look for ways around it.

GREAT LEADERS ARE OPTIMISTS

Optimism and ownership go hand in hand. You must have optimism to see around obstacles and to envision success regardless of the potholes you run across in life . And there will be potholes, believe me. The economy does dip occasionally, and the team might be disturbed by recent events. There may actually be a recruiting crunch. But a great leader knows how to create a positive and enthusiastic environment and overcomes obstacles. Pessimists see obstacles as threatening and something to get angry about. They look for blame and kick butt! To a great leader, obstacles are opportunities and mistakes are learning experiences.

I once read a story about working with mother Teresa. One day her aide sat down to go over the day's progress, Mother Teresa said, "There are so many *problems*. Can't we find a better word to use to describe what is happening?" Several days later, in an airport the colleague had the dubious honor of telling Mother Teresa that they had the "opportunity" to stay in the airport for 8 hours! When you think of an 8 hour layover as an "opportunity," it completely changes your perception of the situation, it changes your attitude and what you might do with your time—especially if you are with Mother Teresa! Are you an optimist? When negative things happen to you, how do you habitually describe them? Do you use optimistic language? Do you learn lessons quickly so they don't happen again? Do you say, "I don't know how" and give up, or do you try to learn something about it? These are the habits of the optimist, and they can be a compass—particularly when the going gets tough.

GREAT LEADERS BRING OUT THE BEST IN OTHERS

Leading today requires a situational approach: "leader for all seasons? In your dreams!" says Tom Peters in an essay for *Fast Company* magazine. Great leaders are the glue that holds the organization together. They are relationship experts and break the "model T" thinking of the past.

Always remember: There is no easy approach to handling people. Being a leader is a challenge to be accepted only by those who are committed to understanding the uniqueness people. How well do you communicate? Are you able to coach people to improve? Do you flex your style to handle a team member's experience level or do you treat everyone exactly the same? Let's look at how leaders produce peak performance in both individuals and the team.

DEVELOPING INDIVIDUAL TEAM MEMBERS

The first lesson for bringing out the best in others is an overall strategy as to how to treat people to create positive expectations. The principle of the self-fulfilling prophecy is: the way a person is treated determines how he or she will behave. Treat people with respect, and let them know you believe they have the potential to achieve great things, and they will be more likely to accomplish their objectives. Never be a "dream stealer." Even when people make mistakes, treat them according to their potential and let them know you expect them to fix the problem or improve next time.

A specific strategy to bring out a person's best is to choose the appropriate leadership style to fit the individual. Do they need a lot of direction or a little? Do they have much experience? How is their confidence? How do you know? To match the appropriate style with each of your people, start by assessing the person's "independence level." and match it with the appropriate style. Use the tool below to guide you in your decision.

Give the person a score of 1-100 in each of the following areas:

Self–Confidence—Team member displays a belief in him/herself, is willing to try new things, is assertive, and displays a positive attitude.

Skill—Team member has demonstrated the ability to perform the job or task to be completed with a minimum training or supervision; is able to complete the job or task within a specified time period. Can solve problems when they arise.

Knowledge—Team member understands the job/task and its impact on the overall team functioning.

Experience—Has a variety of life and work experiences from which to draw to learn, perform, or solve problems.

Add each score for a sum total and divide by 4.

A_____ + B _____ + C_____ + D _____ = _____ divide by 4 = _____

Next choose the appropriate management style according to the numbers below:

1-25—Direct/Instruct—Start at the beginning and take a logical approach to teaching the person what they need to know and do. Tell them what to do, how to do it, and why. Give them structure to instill the confidence to do the job. Checklists, worksheets, analogies and examples are appropriate to guide them toward success. Let them read about the task or watch a video if available. Have regular discussions with them to determine what they are learning and help them through the rough patches. It is a great idea to assess the above four areas to determine in which area to spend the most time. Do you need to build confidence? Knowledge or skill? Or do you need to give the person some experience to move to the next level?

26-65—Coach-Once the person has a clear set of expectations and instructions, they are ready to perform the job. Unfortunately, they may lack experience or practice and have not been able to do it with speed, accuracy or confidence. Let them take on the task and build on what they already know. The coach will give constant performance feedback, so be available to give instructions when needed. Be sure to use a 4:1 ratio of positive to negative feedback. Help them through their mistakes , for they will make many until they master the job. The coach keeps the person moving forward and celebrates success! Remember: Never use a reprimand when a person is in the learning mode—better to set a short-term performance goal.

50-85—Collaborate-At a certain point the team member will have hit the critical point of "discovery" in the job or task. They now know what is expected and how to do it and are able to meet expectations successfully and in a consistent manner. Now is time to back off and let the person take on new assignments on their own. Collaborate with them on goals and expectations. Let them manage their own time and work. Use the facilitation approach more often to help them make their own decisions. Ask questions:

- What are you working on?

- How are you planning to handle that?

- When do you plan to finish the work?

- What can I do to help you?

If the person makes a mistake, they probably realized they were making one in the midst of making it! Let them tell you what happened. Avoid the need to coach and simply begin asking questions:

- What happened?

- How will you fix it?

- Do you need any help?

- What have you learned?

- How will you do it differently next time?

If they don't have the answers, go back and "Coach" when needed.

85-100—Mentor-Agree to some overall expectations and deadlines and let the person determine how something will be done. Follow up occasionally to let them know you are there. Give advice but let them decide how to approach difficult situations. If they drop the ball, go back to the "Collaborator" approach. This person is independent and able to succeed and to learn on her own and will often let you know when things go wrong after she has fixed them. This team member may be a suitable replacement for you if you are looking for one. She is probably ready for promotion and you will be able to delegate freely to her. Be sure to give enough praise and recognition according to personality, and never micromanage someone at this level.

Great leaders remember to take a flexible approach to bringing out peak performance in their team members. How well do you assess your people? Can you coach? Mentor? Instruct? Collaborate? Where do you need to improve your skills? Make a list of your people. Go through the assessment in this chapter with each one—Then match the number to the appropriate style. Create an action plan to implement the proper strategies with each one and make notes to remind yourself as you work with each person.

DEVELOP YOUR LEADERSHIP ACTION PLAN

Look at the following list of the behaviors of successful leaders. Choose one or two to work on. Set a written goal and create an action plan for how you will enhance your skills in that area. Also, put a star next to the ones that you consider your strengths and capitalize on those as you deal with people.

- I can clearly see where my team will be in 5 years and talk about it often with them.
- I read on my industry or area of interest.
- I feel confident in my ability to lead a team.
- I collaborate with the team to create strategies for achieving goals and share it with others.
- I collaborate with the team in establishing team values
- I cultivate identity in the groups I work with.
- I am generally well known and people enjoy working with me.
- I suggest innovative ways to create or improve on things around me.

- I get people excited about projects.
- I keep a positive attitude at all times.
- I praise progress.
- I praise people more than I criticize.
- I assess a person's level of independence before working with them.
- I give clear instructions to people when needed. I provide structure for people who need it.
- I do not need to control everything people do. I know when to back off.
- People can do things any way they want to as long as they meet the goals. It is not necessary to do it "my way".
- I can easily see a way around obstacles when they arise and work to overcome them rather than using them as an excuse for poor results.
- I am always learning something new and strive to build new better habits constantly.
- I use the language creatively and positively to describe challenges, goals, and vision.
- I understand that each person is motivated differently and study what makes people take action.

LEAD FOR LOYALTY

You now have the simple recipe to lead for loyalty. Start with a vision of the future. Who is the team and where are they going? Help team members to see the future and set specific, measurable goals and objectives to create buy-in. Build their loyalty through collaboration with the team on the action plans that will lead to results. Be sure to keep a positive approach when things go wrong—be an optimist that things will work out and the team will want to be a part of the solution, and celebrate success when the team reaches its targets. Work with team members to help them around obstacles and to help them to grow. You are well equipped to work with each person by determining the "independence level" and then choosing the appropriate management style.

Remember: if you take the time to work on yourself and constantly improve your own skills, the team will also improve and will remain loyal to you as you lead them toward success!

CHAPTER TEN

The Power of Three or More

*Tapping into CARMA™ for Personal
and Professional Prosperity.*

Heidi Richards, MA, CPPM, CLL

Heidi's personal mission is to *"Help Small Businesses Bloom by Growing Great Business Leaders."* International Speaker, Elan'trepreneur, and Author, Heidi is an expert in marketing, customer service, sales, self-promotion, networking, leadership and increasing productivity. All this and Having FUN at Work!

She has written for many major news media including a syndicated column for Balance Magazine (The PMS Principles - Partnering Mentoring Service). Heidi has spoken at many International Conferences in Egypt, the Netherlands, Portugal and the USA. She has been recognized in South Florida with Price Waterhouse UP 'n Comers Award, SWBRJ Small Business Person of the Year Award and Broward's Salute to Business Award. In 1997 the American Business Women's Association named her a **National Top 10 Business Woman**. In 2002 Heidi was named Entrepreneur of the Year and in 2003 - Outstanding Retail Leader.

She is one of less than 200 people to hold the professional designation – AAF. She is Past President of the Florida Speakers Association and Founder/Past President of 10 other organizations including www.Wecai.org.

Heidi Richards, MA, CPPM, CLL
Miramar, FL • 800-966-3336 • www.heidirichards.com

Heidi Richards, MA, CPPM, CLL

The Power of Three or More

Tapping into CARMA™ for Personal and Professional Prosperity.

Wouldn't it be great to have your own hand-picked advisory board or board of directors off which you can bounce ideas, offer solutions to your everyday challenges, motivate and inspire you to greatness? Well, you can! This little known strategy in business has propelled many successful people throughout history to achieve greatness even beyond their wildest expectations. In fact, it can do more for you in a short time than almost any strategy you chose in life. The Power of three or more is just that...powerful! It can enhance your professional life by helping you increase visibility, sales, creativity and the bottom line. It can enhance your personal life by making relationships stronger, more fulfilling and FUN!

Bringing three or more people together to solve challenges, generate ideas and create opportunities has been described as a Mastermind Team or often referred to as a Mastermind Alliance. However, there is more to creating your Mastermind Dream Team than just bringing people together. Much more! This is not about a social club, or business networking group. It is a gathering of like-minded individuals who work together to achieve specific goals in all aspects of life. The power of the Mastermind Alliance will help you break away from self-limiting beliefs and grow through the process of coaching each other. Developing accountability and individual commitment is all part of this process. Surrounding yourself with people you know, like and trust gives you energy and creates the impetus for success. If your future power depends on your current choices, then working your CARMA™ will help you expand your consciousness, your ideas and your perceptions. You can achieve the vision for your career and your life using CARMA™ - to Create Abundant Rewards with your Mastermind Alliance.

Using CARMA™ helps you:

- Gain clarity to become more **Creative**

- Become more focused on what you want to **Accomplish**

- **Recognize** things that may be holding you back

- Inspire change that **Makes** a difference

- Set and **Achieve** goals

Have you ever participated in a brainstorming session? If so, you know that when it comes to solving problems, two heads are better than one. Working with another creates a synergy that doesn't exist when we think on our own. Synergy has been defined as one plus one equals three. If that were true, then a mastermind alliance would be 3^2. So Imagine that three people working together could achieve the potential of nine minds. That's the premise for masterminding. Built on the foundation of trust, confidentiality and harmony, these groups form a collective brain trust to address some of life's greatest challenges.

THROUGHOUT HISTORY, MASTERMINDING HAS BEEN USED TO SOLVE LIFE'S ISSUES

Although the term "masterminding" is fairly new, the concept of tapping into the "master mind" is not. The idea of mastermind alliances gained popularity when Napoleon Hill wrote about it in his book, "Think and Grow Rich." In fact, he devoted the entire first chapter to the subject. He wrote about how he learned of the concept from Andrew Carnegie, the richest self-made man of his time. Carnegie told Hill that his success and accumulation of wealth was due entirely to his mastermind process. Hill studied the lives of nearly 500 of the world's wealthiest men and found that they all belonged to a group of peers with whom they received encouragement, support, knowledge, advice and in many cases contacts.

According to Hill, "the accumulation of great fortunes calls for power, and power is acquired through highly organized and intelligently-directed specialized knowledge, but that knowledge does not necessarily have to be in the possession of the person who accumulates the fortune." He goes on to say the mastermind principle is "the coordination of knowledge and effort of two or more people who work toward a definite purpose, in the spirit of harmony."

CUT YOUR LEARNING CURVE EXPONENTIALLY

Anyone who wants to get on the fast-track setting and achieving goals could use this type of counsel. Once I discovered CARMA™, my goal was to multiply that process by becoming involved in several groups, each focusing on different areas in my own life. But let me tell you how I first became involved in this life changing adventure. Six years ago, I received an invitation to attend a Women's meeting hosted by two very successful women, Darren Blake and Priscilla Marotta. Darren is an Executive with Salomon Smith Barney and Priscilla is a Psychologist, international speaker and author. They had the idea to bring thirteen women together to form Women of Wisdom - WOW™. Intrigued with the title, I showed up. The initial purpose of the group was to create a support system for women of influence and power. It became much more than that. Meeting once a month, we talked about our personal and professional challenges and helped one another to solve many of those challenges. Two of us wrote books, many of us shared contacts and we taught one another. For me, this became the ultimate support group, because they encouraged me to look for my natural father, who I ultimately did find. For those of you who are interested, write to me at www.HeidiRichards.com and I will share it with you.

Priscilla is the author of the book *Power and Wisdom, the New Path for Women*. She used our expertise by profiling us in several of the chapters. (I'm in chapter six J). Her newest endeavor, www.womenofwisdom.com was another result of starting WOW. The initial purpose of WOW™ has changed. We have become such good friends that we now meet socially. This oftentimes happens when the initial goals of the group have been accomplished.

MORE CAN BE ACCOMPLISHED IN LESS TIME

Sandy Grason shared her story with me. She is the author of the soon-to-be-released book, *Finding Me, Journaling to Heal Your Life and Manifest Your Dreams* (www.sandygrason.com). One of her initial goals was to get an endorsement for the book by someone of influence. She had heard about the mastermind process and wanted to start a group of her own. In order to recruit potential women to join with her, she spread the word to her circle of influence. Soon she had recruited three women. They meet weekly in her home for two hours and develop strategies to propel their businesses to a higher plateau. I mentioned that one of Sandy's goals was to get an endorsement for her book. Together her group came up with a strategy to be in the right place at the right time when Mark Victor Hansen was in town speaking at a Science of Mind gathering. She had the opportunity to talk with him briefly and invite him to dinner. He accepted. Because he believed in her project and the whole process of journaling, he wrote a glowing endorsement for her. When I asked her why she feels the mastermind process is such a success, Sandy said "It's because everyone in the mastermind group is there to serve and support one another, giving unconditionally in the group. They willingly apply their knowledge, experience and wisdom to solve one another's objectives."

Another group in which I was invited to participate, was organized by Lori Bergman, a dear friend and colleague. It is a dream team of seven women each focusing on personal and professional prosperity. In just the first five weeks we were together, our members accomplished more than we could have alone.

Lori, the founder, created a new company, www.Americasfitnesstrainertothebrides.com, designed her company brochure, made several key contacts from the members' circle of influence, and landed a significant commercial account. Nancy created a new avenue to promote her skin care company, Maureen developed a kick-butt media kit, Frances got input to redesign her website, and I got some great referrals and introductions in order to place my book, *What's Your OccuPLAYtion™?* in specialty gift shops. We meet weekly for two hours focusing on the challenges of one member each week.

An important aspect of a successful mastermind is accountability. When we share our goals and dreams with others they become more attainable for us. Being involved in a mastermind group helps to achieve those goals because there is a built-in accountability factor that may not be a part of our own experiences. We now have others who hold our "feet to the fire," encouraging us to move forward in the direction of those goals.

FORMATS THAT WORK

There are many different formats for masterminding. Some groups meet weekly, monthly, quarterly, annually and any combination in between. Some meet for an hour, two hours, half day, full day, weekend or even a week. Some meet in person, and others meet online. WOW™ originally met monthly, we now meet two to three times a year. While we still share challenges and provide guidance to one another, it is more one-on-one than in the group. FAME (Females Accessing the Minds of Each other) is an online group I started. We are a group of professional speakers who met in the Netherlands and stay in touch online. We talk about our challenges, share resources and offer advice for topic development and other strategies relating to our business. Although we communicate by e-mail, we plan to meet yearly at the same conference where we originally met. Our next in-person meeting is scheduled for Portugal in the fall.

GETTING STARTED

Why wait until you are invited to join a Mastermind group when you can start one of your own? Getting started isn't difficult. The following steps will help you get the maximum benefits from your mastermind relationships.

1. Have a vision and/or a mission.

The hallmark of a successful mastermind group is one with a clear sense of purpose. Put your vision/mission in writing. Share it with your group. Make sure they either help create or agree with what is created. Everyone in the group must buy-into the purpose for long-term success to be achieved. When Lori Bergman started Tuesdays with Lori, she knew the vision and mission even before she decided on whom to invite. They were written and presented to the group for all to discuss. Each of us agreed with the essence of both and decided that we were on the same path as she. The vision is "This group of women comes together to support each other in creating enlightened wealth through our businesses." The mission is: "To meet with the purpose of growing our businesses; creating new businesses; brainstorming and supporting new ideas and projects for current or new business, discovering our business passion; sharing resources with each other including leads; referrals and contacts when possible and appropriate; allowing us to live and create our business dreams and goals to the degree that our work becomes our play."

2. Choose people who have specialized knowledge or skills you lack.

Enlisting people with very different outlooks strengthens a mastermind group. Think about the types of people who would benefit (mutually) from their participation in the group. Each person must believe in the process and be willing to give as well as get from her or his participation. Make a list of potential members. Select people with similar values and aspirations, involved in a process of continual personal development. You could include people within your organization (internal experts); people in your field whom you respect and admire not in direct competition with you (external experts); people in related fields with similar interests. I am in the floral business so my colleagues might include photographers, caterers, event planners, hoteliers, and the like. Mentors and role models, people who are successful and model the type of professional behavior you wish to emulate, are other categories to consider. Power sources such as clients, prospects, friends, and people connectors could help create your dream team. And finally make sure there are challengers in your group. Challengers are those people who you trust to be honest with you and not "yes" you to death - - doing so in a way that you can accept and learn from.

3. Personally contact each person and invite them to a meeting.

Set a time and place to meet. Many people still have not experienced the mastermind process so you may be required to give an overview of your goals in putting the group together.

4. Make a time commitment and stick to it.

As I mentioned earlier, the best format is the one with which everyone agrees and to which they are willing to commit time. If people are not committed to the process, to giving, to growth, to the group, they quickly leave. In order to achieve true success, there must be commitment. When you make the commitment, don't allow anything except serious emergencies to interfere with your date. Meeting regularly encourages bonding and the group quickly gains momentum.

5. Rules of Engagement.

Establish an agenda and follow it. The agenda can be formal (written) or informal (implied). An agenda creates a sense of order during the meetings. Set the agenda around issues and challenges. A typical agenda might include open discussion at the beginning of the meeting and then focusing on individual challenges for a set period of time. My in-person groups focus on one member's challenge each meeting with the other members offering feedback and advice. Each member gets his or her turn to share. This is very powerful because each of us learns something from the others' challenges. My online group (FAME) meets in a "chat room" and we each (there are four of us) ask a question or share a challenge we are having. Each person, in turn, responds.

During any brainstorming time, we follow the rules of cooperation in the spirit of harmony. No judgment, just ideas, quantity vs. quality, etc. We then discuss and discard those ideas that we feel will not move us toward our goals. At the end of the meeting we have a share session and open discussion. This time generates incredible synergy within the group. Give one another a homework assignment, which encourages accountability. Make the meetings fun. You can start with a motivational reading, and share successes. End on a high note as well.

6. Keep it small and simple.

Groups of 3 to 10 work best. More than that and you may find two meetings going on at the same time.

7. Decide on a policy for disclosure at the very beginning.

My in-person groups openly discuss details of our respective businesses with the understanding that "inside secrets" are never discussed outside our group. The online group is not as open online. If we have a serious issue, we make a point of calling each other and discussing our issues off-line.

8. Consider a facilitator.

A facilitator who keeps the group on target and on task. Take turns. You learn to facilitate by doing. The facilitator can also be the organizer for planning his or her meeting.

9. Leave your ego at the door.

This is not the place to try to impress others or act high and mighty. Humility is the greatest teacher. Although we want to look good to the rest of the world, in a mastermind group you should be able to admit anything without fear of penalty. Trust deepens as we allow ourselves to be open and honest with one another.

10. Know when to call it quits.

If you aren't making a difference to the others or they aren't making a difference to you, find another group. When the mastermind no longer meets your needs, you no longer need to meet.

Helen Keller said, "Alone we can do so little, together we can do so much!" When I think of all the goals I have aspired to and achieved, it often overwhelms me. I am so grateful for the many people who have helped me to discover CARMA™ and get from where I was to where I am today.

CHAPTER ELEVEN

It's Not About the Money – It's About Me

Finding job satisfaction through personal priorities.

Janis E. Stewart

A math major with an art scholarship, Jan spent 30 years in "corporate America" trying to figure out what she would do "when she grew up."

She now owns her own outsourcing and consulting business where she applies her "Girl Friday" skills, accounting training and human resources experience.

In 2002, Jan published *Newsletters – Putting It All Together*, the first in "A Bitty Book of Basics" series. She is currently working on *One Plus One Always Equals Two – Bookkeeping for Those Who Hate Math*.

Janis E. Stewart
Lawrence, KS • 785-843-8521 • www.officehelpline.com

Janis E. Stewart

It's Not About the Money –
It's About Me

Finding job satisfaction through personal priorities.

Today's working women have won many battles. Some have even won the "war" and are now in powerful, well-paying jobs. But are we happy?

In this new millennium, career women no longer feel locked in to choosing either "playing with the boys" or "being on the mommy track." Priorities are being analyzed. Goals are being re-evaluated. Some women are reaffirming that they are doing what really makes them happy. Others are job-sharing or choosing lateral, even lesser, positions when making job changes. An increasing number are starting their own businesses – putting in excessive hours without complaint (or guaranteed financial rewards). Regardless of the direction we choose, personal job satisfaction is gaining importance.

We are finally allowing our hearts to help us make satisfying career choices. We are no longer locked into the old thinking that success is based solely on money or perceived status and power. Personal values are now being considered when establishing career success benchmarks. Our career success benchmarks can now include our need to do something fun, something interesting or something that helps others.

IS IT TIME FOR A CHANGE?

Are you ready for a change? Consider some of the possible signs.

- You are tired when you begin your day and you have felt this way so long you are starting to think it is "normal."

- You have the "trying to quit crabbies" and you don't even smoke (or you aren't trying to quit)!

- "Happy" and "fun" are words you can only relate to child-hood.

- You are experiencing extreme dental pain. Your dentist confirms you have no real problems but recommends a bite block for your frequent jaw clenching.

- Your spouse asks if you would like to take a vacation with the "girls" this year. You can't remember the last time you took a real vacation or spent any time with your girlfriends. You are not even sure you have any girlfriends left to call.

In the early stages of the job I left, I thought I deserved more money. Later I realized money, although I still felt it justified, would not compensate for the real issues at hand. I was experiencing most of the health symptoms described above. Although my husband didn't ask about separate vacations, I'm sure he would have liked to send me somewhere. I was also ignoring other physical problems, including weight gain and migraines – assuring myself they were all normal symptoms of "getting older."

I actually went to my physician, convinced I was peri-menopausal. He assured me everything was fine. "So why do I want to kill somebody?" I demanded, eyeing him as my next victim. He provided no real answers and his nurse advised me to "pull up my boot straps." This would pass.

The following year when I went in for my physical, my doctor proudly announced (referring to menopause), "Well, we dodged that bullet." What? The one aimed at your head? I was thinking as I replied, "Yes. Amazing what happens when you quit a job." I respect my physician and trust his medical abilities, but he had addressed only the medical possibilities. In actuality, conflict with my job was what was literally making me sick.

As someone who generally chooses flight over fight, I was fortunate. A friend offered me a short-term training position. It was my open door and I took it. The day I gave notice, my boss (recognizing an unfulfilled promise) asked, "Is it about the money?" My response was, "Not any more." It wasn't about the money. A pay increase would have only served to tighten the "golden handcuffs," but not resolve the real issues of fulfillment and self-worth.

You may not be experiencing the physical ailments I described or other signs of burnout, but ask yourself the following questions:

- Despite your requests for more responsibility and job development, have you been able to learn anything new in the past year?

- Has your job caused you to give up important family events or other quality time (community or religious activities)?

- Are you bored with your job or simply not challenged by it any longer?

- Is your workload exhausting and never-ending?

- Are you treated with respect?

- Do you find it hard to get up in the morning (or difficult to go to sleep at night)?

- Do you lack energy or excitement for your work?

- Are you abusing substances (such as alcohol)?

Answering yes to these questions is an indication you need a change.

WHAT WILL IT TAKE TO MAKE YOU HAPPY?

You may have asked or been asked the "happy" question many times before. "What will it take to make you happy?" is posed by frustrated parents to despondent children and even frustrated supervisors to sullen employees. But have you asked yourself that question? If you have, have you honestly answered it?

In May, 2003, CareerWomen.com released the results of a two-week poll on job satisfaction. Of the several hundred respondents, 72% of the women were not inspired by their work. When asked what would inspire job satisfaction, an overwhelming 94% sited respect.

Professor Andrew Oswald from University of Warwick says, "The whole trick of being happy is getting your aspirations in line with your potential achievements." If you have dared to say, "I'm not happy" you have probably been told "life's not fair" or to "get over it." These, along with all the other clichés, are not satisfactory responses. Nor is the famous, "So what's it going to take? More money?" Money may buy lots of things, but today's women realize it truly doesn't buy happiness. The key is job satisfaction (which may in turn bring more money).

YOU REALLY THOUGHT YOU MADE A GOOD CAREER CHOICE.

You are not the same woman you were ten years ago or even last year. The more you experience, the more you change and the better you understand yourself. Your values and motivators change with time and life events. Things you once felt strongly about may not be priorities now. It is better to make conscious choices rather than let your career "just happen."

Dream Job Coaching of Oakland, California, found only a small percentage of people are actually working in the field in which they initially obtained a degree. Why? In many instances these individuals chose the "Career Du Jour" – getting a degree in a field perceived to have the best job opportunities at the time – without analyzing their true desires. They chose money (job opportunities) over happiness (true desires).

The Bureau of Labor Statistics reports 7 out of 10 Americans don't like their jobs. Yet, many stay. They stay because they are in a comfort zone with familiar faces, routine tasks or a salary on which they can survive. They stay because they are afraid to leave.

If things are so bad, then why do we keep working? Al Gini, in his book *My Job, My Work*, tells us that adults need work for the same reason children need play – for fulfillment. Gini says our careers "become our mark of identity, our signature on the world." Beyond the need for money, we are compelled to work for self-expression and a feeling of accomplishment.

After examining who you are and where you are, you may find fear of lost identity becomes your motivation for change. Becoming pro-active and changing jobs may be the catalyst needed to improve your self-esteem and increase your job satisfaction. Determine what makes you happy. Identify what is important to YOU (family, self, community, relationships, finance). Start with the big picture; then work out the smaller details.

Key areas for self-evaluation are people, data and things. Ask yourself the following questions – and write down your answers:

- What are you good at? What do others ask you to do for them?

- What do you volunteer to do?

- How do you use your free time?

- Do you like to fix things or just take them apart to see how they work?

- To what organizations do you belong? Which ones provide you the greatest personal satisfaction?

- What pushes your hot buttons (positively and negatively)?

- Are there political, social or environmental issues about which you feel strongly?

Remember, no effort is required to get somewhere in life, but to get somewhere meaningful you need to decide where you want to go, then make a plan to get there.

PLAN BEFORE YOU LEAP.

The first step toward career satisfaction is taking responsibility for your future. Before you make major career changes, you need a clear vision of who you are and where you want to go. Then make a plan for getting there. "Plan your work and work your plan." These words of wisdom from Mary Kay Ash, founder of Mary Kay Cosmetics, hold true in every field of endeavor. This is your dream; make your own plan (not someone else's) with your own goals and expectations.

As you develop your plan:

1. Set goals. Make sure they are SMART goals.

   - Specific

   - Measurable

   - Achievable

   - Realistic

   - Time-bounded

2. Identify your transferable skills and determine ways to obtain additional skills needed. This may include taking on "stretch" assignments at your current job – those tasks that place you on the edge and force you to grow your skill level.

3. Maintain life-work balance. This may require "containerizing" – doing what you intend to do, when you intend to do it, for as long as you intend to do it, then STOPPING!

4. Build a network of contacts. What you know is important, but who you know may get you your dream job.

5. Volunteer. You can build invaluable skills and contacts as a volunteer.

6. Target companies offering positions that match your goals (even if they are not currently hiring) and learn all you can about them.

7. Never lose site of who you are and what is important to you.

    • Your life and career history

    • Appreciation of your accomplishments

    • Your special knowledge, skills and abilities

    • Your interests

    • Your ever-changing motivations and needs

As you develop your plan, you may discover ways to improve job satisfaction in your current position. If you can, terrific. Continue to "work your plan," however, as the fix may not completely meet your needs. Remember, you are the one in control.

IS JOB SATISFACTION REALLY THAT BIG A DEAL?

Max Messmer, chairman and CEO of Robert Half International, Inc., reports 70% of employees are less motivated today than they used to be. An amazing 80% report they could perform significantly better if they wanted. 50% say they only put in enough effort to keep their jobs. Is this job satisfaction? What does it take to motivate today's employees?

In his book, *Motivating Employees for Dummies*, Messmer sites six key motivators:

- Positive work environment

- Communicating and fostering open communication

- Advancement

- Competitive compensation package

- Reward and recognition

- Teamwork and collaboration

Messmer's list shows it takes more than a "compensation (money or perks) package" to be motivated. It takes a "job satisfaction package." It is up to you to prioritize the elements that provide you with job satisfaction.

ESTABLISHING YOUR PERSONAL PRIORITIES.

By better understanding yourself, getting in touch with your interests, and recognizing your accomplishments, you can develop a clearer picture of what is really important to you and begin working in the that direction.

Traditionally, people are matched to jobs based on abilities, interests and values. Consideration should also be given to:

- Involvement with others – your personal need to work with others (extrovert) or work alone (introvert).

- Natural awareness (what you tend to notice) – facts and details (sensor) or connections and relationships (intuitive).

- Decision making style – thinker or feeler.

- Action preference – structured or spontaneous.

- Environment – structured and orderly (judger) or open and adapting (perceiver).

- Personality style – director, thinker, relater or socializer.

These are core items as to who you are and what will work for you, whereas, your "big three" traditional qualities change with age and experience.

Your age also plays a large role in how you look at yourself and your career. Old thinking defined a job as what a person did to pay the bills and support a family while hobbies and home life were what a person did for fulfillment and personal identity. Today, we feel work should be fulfilling. We also realize it should be more than "just a paycheck" because it plays a key role in identifying who we are.

CAN YOU FIND JOB SATISFACTION AND STILL PAY THE BILLS?

You've dreamed about your perfect job. You know what type of work you would be doing, the type of people you would be working with and how you would spend your perfect day. You've even considered where it would be located. Now, how do you find the balance between following your heart (your dream job) and keeping a roof over your head? Consider multiple jobs.

Try shedding the old thinking that someone who has two or more jobs is "under-employed," doesn't have a "real" job, or can't "make it" in her chosen career. Holding multiple jobs can be your perfect solution. You can pursue jobs that satisfy your personal needs (many of which were once considered "hobbies") while holding "traditional" positions to meet your financial needs. This method may also prove to be your transition into self-employment as your dream job may be one that grows into a self-supporting business.

IT'S NOT ABOUT THE MONEY.

Discover yourself. Make your own benchmarks for success. Develop a plan and put it into action. Continue to evaluate your motivators and values in relation to your position(s).

You may find your motto going from "Thank goodness, it's Friday!" to "My goodness, it's Friday?" as your career satisfaction level increases. Once you stop focusing on money you may realize your job does not define you. You define it. You can then find significance in what you do. And when you ask yourself "Is it worth it?" the "it" will represent your investment of time and energy – not money.

CHAPTER TWELVE

What About ME?

How to get the recognition you deserve.

Cynthia B. Stotlar, M.Ed., SPHR

"Employees are frustrated not knowing how to set themselves up for greater responsibilities and/or promotion. Promotional opportunities are fewer and farther between now with recent downsizings and the flattening of organizations over the past decade. However, promotions are still there for those who are willing to work diligently on their skills." says Cynthia Stotlar.

As a business consultant, author and national speaker, Cynthia helps businesses select, train and retain star performers. This improves the business' productivity and profitability. Cynthia works with management to design superior employee selection and retention processes. She provides management development to enhance the people management skills so that they retain their star performers. Cynthia also works with employees so they can become better team players and provide excellent internal and external customer service. Her areas of expertise include

- Building Dynamite Teams
- Retaining Star Performers
- Becoming Great Team Players
- Providing Superior Customer Service
- Rewards & Recognition on a Shoestring
- Maximizing Work Relationships

Creative Business Solutions
Topeka, KS • 800-635-2310 • www.cbsks.com

Cynthia B. Stotlar, M.Ed., SPHR

What About ME?

How to get the recognition you deserve.

If you want to set yourself up for success within your current company, this chapter is for you. The ability to sell yourself and your ideas is instrumental to your success. You may be doing a dynamite job, but if no one notices, they won't realize your potential and YOU won't get promoted. Promotional opportunities are fewer and farther between now with the downsizings and flattening of organizations over the past decade, but they are still there for those who are willing to work diligently on their skills.

This chapter looks at ways to let others know of your ideas and successes. When you use these techniques, management will come to see you as a team player, a creative thinker and a problem solver who is promotable.

First a question: Do you get the recognition you deserve now?

If you answered no, let's delve a bit deeper and do a personal gap analysis. How do you want to be perceived in the following areas by others? How do you think you are being perceived right now? Is there a gap?

- Team player?
- Dependable - Reliable?
- Creative?
- Problem solver?
- Assertive?

- High quality work?
- Effective?
- Efficient?
- Trustworthy?

What we perceive to be, we believe to be.

Who's to say what's true - you or me?

Perception is reality for the person perceiving it. So if your manager doesn't perceive you are promotable, then right now you aren't. But you CAN work to CHANGE that perception.

5 WAYS TO GET THE RECOGNITION YOU DESERVE

If you work on these 5 things, you WILL become more promotable in the eyes of management.

- Know Your VITAL Statistics

- Get CLOSE to Your Customers

- PROPOSE to Your Boss

- Promote OTHERS' Successes

- TOOT Your Own Horn

1ST: KNOW YOUR VITAL STATISTICS

Take a moment and complete the "KNOWLEDGE CHECKLIST"
K = know this
D = don't know this

K D MANAGEMENT

❑ ❑ What are our goals for the next 3 months? 6 months? year?

❑ ❑ What problems should be addressed immediately?

❑ ❑ Are there any on-going projects that need work in the next 3 months?

K D   PRODUCT/SERVICE KNOWLEDGE

❑ ❑   What does my work unit produce?

❑ ❑   Who uses the product(s) or service?

❑ ❑   How long does it take to produce each product or service?

❑ ❑   How many products or services can we produce per day? Week? Month? Year?

❑ ❑   How many complaints do we get per product or service?

❑ ❑   What is the error rate per product or service?

❑ ❑   What are the costs per product or service?

K D   EMPLOYEE KNOWLEDGE

❑ ❑   What are the primary responsibilities of each employee?

❑ ❑   What special projects are being done and by whom?

❑ ❑   What seems to be working well?

❑ ❑   What are the improvement opportunities?

K D   PEERS

❑ ❑   What do other departments think of the work unit?

❑ ❑   What seems to work well? What needs improvement?

❑ ❑   Who are the decision-makers?

❑ ❑   Who are good resources for budgeting? Employee issues? Production issues?

Now ask yourself: "Are there any areas where I don't know the answers?" If so, any you didn't know is a prime area where you can improve. The more you know about what your manager's goals and expectations are, the more likely you are to make choices that support those goals and expectations. That makes for a very happy manager! And a happy manager is much more fun to work with!

The more you know about the products or services you provide, the easier it is to identify opportunities for improvement. Then document improvements you have made in productivity, revenue and customer service. This is a great way to prove your worth to the company and get that promotion.

You can do this by keeping track of how long it takes to perform a task now, how you can do in a day, and what the overall cost per task is. Then brainstorm ways to make the task more efficient, easier, or less costly. Show management your ideas, get permission to try the new method, and then test it. There are times it's easier to get forgiveness than permission, so you will have to make the call on your immediate manager's outlook on the implementation of your idea.

Typically, management LOVES employees who research and present ideas that could help the department. Your promotability level will rise sharply.

Personal Action Steps

To develop a better knowledge base of my vital statistics, I need to know:

_____

_____

_____

2ND: GET CLOSE TO YOUR CUSTOMERS

Customer service is crucial in every business. What happens if you don't deliver high quality service to the external customer? Business declines and you are out looking for a new job. Well, internal customer service is every bit as important as external customer service. Kenneth Blanchard and Ron Zemke, two customer service experts, estimate that approximately 30-40% of external customer service problems are a direct result of internal customer service breakdowns.

If you are good at providing solid internal AND external customer service, you will stand out from your peers. Find out what your customers expect from you and your work unit. How? By simply asking.

A concept from Blanchard's book *Creating Raving Fans*, is to meet with your customers to share your goals and your vision for your work or department. Ask about their goals and ideas as well. Then together develop a vision of what customer service should look like.

It is a great way to open communication and to develop a greater appreciation for each person's responsibilities and the challenges they face. An easy way to start this dialogue is to invite your customer to lunch.

Look for ways to "wow" your customers.

Zemke, in *Delivering Knock Your Socks Off Service*, says we need to provide service that is convenient, timely, consistent, dependable, and professionally delivered. Plus, we need to be assessable, responsive, and courteous.

Ask yourself:

How can I deliver service that is...
More convenient? _____
More timely? _____
More consistent? _____
More dependable? _____
More professionally delivered? _____

How can I be...
More accessible? _____
More responsive? _____
More courteous? _____

Problem solve collaboratively with your customers.

All too often a complaint is made by a customer and the department solves it without involving the complainant. Rarely, does it work. Being open to problem solving together shows a tremendous strength on your part and will get you a better solution every time. Try it!

Personal Action Steps

To get closer to my internal customers, I need to:

_____
_____
_____

To get closer to my external customers, I need to:

_____
_____
_____

3RD: PROPOSE TO YOUR BOSS

No, this doesn't mean you should get down on bended knee and ask for your manager's hand in marriage. But DO propose changes in the way work is done if that change would increase revenue, customer service, employee retention, accuracy or quality, etc. If you did steps 2 and 3 in this chapter, you have ideas to propose. Now it is time to sell them!

Do you consider yourself to be in sales? You should be answering an enthusiastic YES!!! Every time you have an idea, you join the sales force. Here's a 6-step approach to a sales pitch for your ideas.

1. Brainstorm...Ask yourself (and others) what could be done in your department (or organization) that would increase revenue, customer service, employee retention, product accuracy or quality, and/or save time.

2. Research...Find out exactly what your department's goals are for the year so you can show how your idea will help meet the goals. Determine "what's in it for management" so they take your ideas and run with it. Get specific information on what costs or time that would be saved or exactly how things would improve. Then review successful proposals your peers have previously submitted so you can determine the right format.

3. Plan...Think through the process, and develop your objectives in relation to those of the organization and department. Include an effectiveness measure (unit cost, length of time). Write out the benefits that management will derive from your plan as well as your own area's benefits. Remember, everyone wants to know "what's in it for me." Have lower budget options available so if pushed, you can negotiate.

4. Prepare... Provide an executive overview in the proposal and include charts and graphs if appropriate. Proofread twice. Be comfortable with your research so you can field questions. Anticipate questions your management team will ask and have answers ready along with evidence to support your claims. Then pick the right time to present your idea.

5. Present...Start your presentation with an overview of the idea and the how management would benefit by adopting the idea. Then review the details. Be calm but enthusiastic. Ask for questions. Have any forms that need signing, like purchase orders etc., with you in case you get a quick yes. Always thank everyone for his/her time.

6. Follow-up...Report results.

Personal Action Steps

I want to pitch ideas on ways we can:

_____

_____

_____

4TH: PROMOTE OTHERS' SUCCESSES

Everyone wants to be recognized and to feel valued. The more you make others feel recognized and valued, the more they will value you. Do it publicly whenever possible. Use staff meetings to say thanks to peers. Buy blank cards, use commercial greeting cards or make your own "trademark" cards

Congratulate others for...
- a job well done
- an idea
- a project completed
- a promotion

Thank others for their...
- assistance
- support
- latitude
- encouragement

Personal Action Steps

I need to congratulate _____

for _____

I need to thank_____

for _____

5TH: TOOT YOUR OWN HORN

Do you write regular reports to your boss?

If you get an annual performance appraisal (and most of us do), you should write a monthly update report at least. These are great for letting your immediate manager know what you've accomplished. They also make great supporting documentation when asking for a raise or promotion or at performance appraisal time.

So write "success" stories regularly. Be sure to talk in ways that make management listen such as return on investment, savings, specific improvements, errors reduced, etc.

Example:

Working collaboratively with two other departments, our new program has been implemented on time and within budget! In the first month, we saved $1,500.00 over our previous practice by improving our turnaround time by 2 days per transaction.

As you know, we have identified a problem regarding the initial training program. After discussing this with the staff, I have begun to develop a training module. It will be ready for the next group. Hopefully, that will solve the problem. I will review a draft of the training module with you next week at your convenience.

This example report says: Look what I've done...

- I work well with others.

- I've organized my routine work to carry out this extra project

- I can meet deadlines

- I can save the organization money

- I can problem solve with others

- I have initiative

Personal Action Steps

I can toot my own horn more effectively by:

_____

_____

_____

If you focus on improving in these five areas, you will get the recognition you deserve! And with that recognition will come promotional opportunities.

In today's flatter organizations, promotional opportunities are fewer and farther between so also keep your mind open to lateral moves that would increase your knowledge or skills. This can ultimately increase your promotability. It definitely makes you more valuable to the company you work in now and more marketable to other companies.

CHAPTER THIRTEEN

Cranial Aerobics

Powerful play for professional progress.

Vicki Trembly

Vicki Trembly is an author, speaker, comic and improv actor. She is a founding member of Topeka Civic Theatre's Improvisational Comedy Company, Laughing Matters. She noticed that the skills used by improv actors are pretty handy in coping with the challenges of real life. Using the games and exercises that help make her successful on stage Vicki developed Cranial Aerobics.

Vicki incorporates her experiences as a comic, talk show host, care-giver, promoter, and sales rep to present a dynamic, high energy workout that will improve creativity, enhance communication skills, reduce stress, and encourage bondage through laughter.

William Shakespeare said, "all the world is a stage". The secret is no one wakes up with a script under their pillow. Life is improv. It isn't always a comedy, but with good cranial conditioning you can make your own personal play more interesting and fun.

Vicki Trembly Presents...
Topeka, KS • 785-224-5408 • www.cranialaerobics.com

<u>Vicki Trembly</u>

Cranial Aerobics

Powerful play for professional progress.

Whether you are the head of a major corporation or the head of a household, the ability to find creative solutions is an important asset. We are all born creative. Ask a child how the lamp got broken. You might hear a fantastic story about how a giant purple crocodile knocked it over with his tail. Give him a big empty box and it will become a time machine, a house, a car. But somewhere on our journey to adulthood, we crawl into the box and stay there.

People become very set in their thinking. When they don't HAVE to find new ways to do things or see solutions in new ways, they continue to do the same things in the same ways and often end up doing the same job for years. Exercising your brain with play can help new ideas come more easily. In this chapter you will learn to improve your creative thinking skills with Cranial Aerobics.

Cranial Aerobics will help you become:

- An exceptional communicator and negotiator
- More spontaneous
- A more skillful leader
- More inventive
- Physically healthier
- More confident
- Mentally stronger
- More aware of possibilities

More than ever before, businesses are looking for creative workers. In an effort to find these workers, many companies are replacing standard resume questions with brain teasers and puzzles as a way to find resourceful, innovative workers. Microsoft asks, "How are M&M's made?" Or, "What is the height of the Empire State Building in quarters and what would be the total dollar amount of these coins?" Or "If you are on a boat, and you throw your suitcase overboard, will the water level rise or fall?" They aren't looking for a correct answer. They are looking to see how you process information and how you deal under pressure.

Actor/comedian John Cleese, an expert on creativity in the workplace, says that if businesses want creative workers they must give them time to play. Play isn't the same as learning. Learning involves categorizing and memorizing facts. Play keeps your brain sharp and flexible by using it in new ways. Play expands your mind helping you to link the facts that you already know in unusual ways.

Play has another benefit. In involves healthy doses of laughter. Laughter is also a powerful bonding agent. The primary Darwinian function of laughter is to act as social glue. In their hiring interviews, Southwest Airlines asks, "When was the last time you laughed at yourself?" And the answer IS important.

You may have seen a popular television show called "Whose Line is it Anyway?." In the show actors are given characters and a location and asked to create a scene on the spot. This is really not that much different than real life. The characters in your scene are your co-workers; the location is your workplace.

In rehearsals (yes, they do rehearse) the actors put themselves in ridiculous situations and work within outlandish limitations to force their minds to be adaptable and intuitive. I created Cranial Aerobics by modifying these games and exercises for non-performance use.

THE 4 BASIC RULES OF CRANIAL AEROBICS

1. Don't deny

2. Take a risk

3. No hesitations, and most importantly

4. Have fun.

Cranial Aerobics is meant first and foremost to be fun. It's okay to have fun, even in the workplace. Especially in the work place.

Okay, I see you peeking out of your box. Are you ready to come out and play?

These first exercises are designed to be done solo and can be done any time and almost anywhere. Use them to shake loose the cobwebs over your morning coffee or to restart your creative engine during the day.

For the writing exercises, I want you to write with your wrong hand. By using the wrong hand your brain creates new dendrites. You should take every opportunity to develop dendrites. They are the connecting tendrils that pass information from cell to cell in your brain. The more you have the easier it is to retrieve the information you have and the easier it is to acquire new information. Recent studies suggest that dendrites help in the fight against Alzheimer's and age-related dementia.

Another thing I am going to ask you to do is to create your own personal "Noodle Dance". Marilyn Albert, a brain researcher at Harvard University, says dancing, particularly square dancing, ballet, tap and line dancing, aids small blood vessels and increases oxygen to the brain. Movement can influence your thought process. Have you ever had a great idea during a workout? Do you ever take a walk to help you figure something out? That's because when your body is free, your mind can wander free as well.

If you have young children you may be familiar with the 'Noodle Dance". Whenever Peanut, Butter or Jelly, the lead characters in the Disney cartoon PB&J Otter, have a problem to figure out they all do the "Noodle Dance" and by the end of the dance, they have a solution.

Your "Noodle Dance" doesn't have to be elaborate. Just let your body move. Add a do-si-do or a couple of pirouettes and stretch to your own internal music for a few seconds. If you feel stuck during any of the exercises, do your Noodle Dance. After you complete each exercise, you can do your own congratulatory dance. You can even sing if you are so inclined.

CRANIAL CONNECTIONS

Equipment: Paper, pencil, and printed material.

Cranial Connections is a gentle warm up that will stretch your brain like a rubber band, and like a rubber band, once it is stretched, it won't return to its original size. The connections you form will remain open, enhancing the flow of communication between brain cells.

Choose a random noun. For example, box. Write down all the words you associate with the word box. I thought of...

- box set
- box turtle
- man in the box
- Boxer rebellion
- boxed in
- x-box
- ring box
- boxy

- box springs
- Candlebox
- boxing ring
- black box
- box your ears
- outside the box
- jack in the box

Take a minute or so. Let your mind out to wander around and find as many associations as you can. They don't have to make sense or be spelled correctly. For the word tree I used tree-mendous and Sarah Coven-tree. They just have to work for you.

I'll start you off with a few words. Then pick your own random words from a book or newspaper. Remember to write with your wrong hand.

Snow_____

_____

_____

Cookie_____

_____

_____

Bat_____

_____

_____

Mist_____

_____

_____

Flower(flour)_____

_____

_____

FAKING IT

Equipment: Paper, pencil, and magazine.

During sales training at Cumulus Broadcasting, it was recommended that we read industry magazines pertaining to our clients. That way you could talk intelligently about their product and concerns. During an interview with the owner of a large hotel chain I mentioned that I had read they were opening a new "store" in a few months. He was impressed. From an article in Hotel Magazine I had learned that insiders call their properties stores. It was a small thing but it showed that I cared enough to learn the lingo. I got the account.

Often the information would just get stored away. But sometime in the future it would rise to the surface. Sometimes it helped me make a connection to another client or industry. Sometimes I just got a W.H.I.M. A Wildly Hysterical Inspirational Moment. When a client told me he was implementing a Matrix system in his business, my first thought that he was going to make all his employees use the same shampoo or learn to dodge bullets in slow motion. Then I remembered reading in a computer magazine that Matrix referred to a computer program.

A few times a week, browse through magazines on different subjects that are not related to your field or interest. There are hundreds of magazines on any subject you can imagine. Your local library has a huge variety available. Flip through one while you're in line at the store. You can even find some magazines on-line. You don't have to become an expert on the subject. You're just trying to pick up a new word or idea. Write down what you learn. Again, with your wrong hand. That single thought may trigger ideas or bring back memories that have been stored away for years. Perhaps it will lay dormant, waiting for the chance to pop into your head at just the right moment.

YOU NAME IT

Equipment: Ten random objects.

I like to play this game with small toys. You can use office supplies or other household objects in your vicinity. You'll need at least 10 things you can pick up or touch. The reason for this is that the mind/body connection is very powerful. This Cranial Aerobics exercise strengthens your creative ability by forcing the separation of your mind/body connection.

Spread the items on a table in front of you. Pick up each thing and name it. Fast. Don't name it anything that it could actually be. For example, your stapler cannot be called 'stapler'. But you could call it apple, or Minnesota, or Aunt Hilda. Also no serial naming like Toyota – Dodge - Plymouth. Go fast, don't hesitate, or say uumm. If you do, start over.

If you can do all ten items the first time you try this, you didn't go fast enough. Speed is the key to this exercise. You'll find it very difficult at first. Who am I kidding? I've played this for over 10 years and it's always tough. That's why I use toys; they are non- breakable. It is fun and extremely effective in creating new connections in the brain.

DEVIATED DICTIONARY

Equipment: Paper, pencil, and dictionary.

The next exercise is both educational and creative.

Flip through a dictionary and choose a word at random. Read the word, spell it aloud and read the definition. Use the word in a sentence. That's the educational part. Now with your wrong hand write the word down, spelling it backwards. Say this new word aloud and define it. I chose the word "inebriate". Backwards, it became "etairbeni". I decided that etairbeni is a noun meaning "a hat decorated with chocolate éclairs". For my sentence I used, "I bought a new etairbeni for Easter and gained ten pounds."

Deviated Dictionary will not only expand your vocabulary, it will help your imaginative and descriptive skills.

GROUP ACTIVITIES

Of course you can use any of the above exercises in a group. Leadership is a highly prized asset in today's business world. using Cranial Aerobics exercises in your team meetings or during a coffee break with your co-workers will induce laughter. Laughter opens the door to more real and risky communication. These Cranial Aerobics activities will break down barriers and form new bonds within your group.

LAST LETTER

Equipment: None.

This exercise improves your communication skills by forcing you to listen on multiple levels during a conversation. This works best in groups of two or three. Introduce a topic. It can be one that is of concern to everyone, or used as an ice breaker topic like "your favorite vacation spot". Instruct the participants that after the first sentence, all subsequent replies and interactions to the conversation MUST start with the last letter of the previous sentence.

So Betty starts by saying, "Last year we went to Bar Harbor."

Maggie could say, "Really, I've always wanted to go there. Where did you stay?"

Betty might reply, "You know we had an RV and we slept in the Mall parking lot."

Then Carly could chime in with, "This year I'm going back to Lake Shawnee."

It works best if you set up a goal to be met. Let the group play for a couple of minutes so every one has a chance to participate.

You can use this as a solo exercise with anyone by making all your replies begin with the last letter of the other persons sentence. It will make telemarketing calls a workout for your head.

TEN THINGS THAT START WITH "P"

Equipment: Medium sized stuffed toy.

This is a fun and simple game that will improve your ability to think under pressure. This works best with a group of 6-10 players. Have the group form a circle with one person in the center. The person in the center shuts her eyes and the players in the circle begin passing the toy clockwise. I like to have the group sing their favorite commercial jingle as they do this. The center person says "STOP", opens her eyes, points to the person holding the toy, and says a letter. The person holding the toy immediately passes the toy counterclockwise and tries to say ten words that start with that letter before the toy makes it around the circle. If she can't, she takes her place in the center and the former center person joins the circle.

This sounds so simple. The letter is not always "P". All letters are eligible. "Q's" and "Z's" are very exciting. But you will be surprised at how difficult thinking of ten words that start with "T" is when you see a fluffy pink cat coming toward you.

I hope you enjoyed your Cranial Aerobics workout. Cranial Aerobics is good for your mind and your body. Your brain is a muscle. It will atrophy without use. Laughing gives your stomach the same kind of workout as sit-ups. The physical and mental benefits of these exercises will last long after the laughter has subsided. It's easy to train you brain to be creative with Cranial Aerobics. Like the little girl in the commercial says, "grown-ups need recess too"! Can you come out and play?

CHAPTER FOURTEEN

Working in Your Bunny Slippers

The secrets of working from home and loving it!

DJ Watson

DJ Watson is a Professional Speaker and business owner with a favorite saying: "Eat a toad in the morning and nothing worse will happen to you the rest of the day." Her mission is to help you find the "toads" taking over your life causing stress, guilt and overwhelm.

As a speaker, she shares ready-to-use tips in her lively talks that enable you to take back control, get organized and still maintain your sanity.

As a business owner, she provides time and sanity saving options to busy professionals via her Virtual Assistant Agency at www.VitalAssistant.com and www.VirtualMVP.com. DJ and her consortium of Vital Assistants, provide marketing and business support for solo-entrepreneurs.

No stranger to unusual work environments, DJ founded her parent company sorganized® Professional Business Operations in 1994. Prior to this, DJ spent 10 years overseas as a senior Executive for the USO Europe and Middle East – including deployments to Desert Storm and Somalia in support of our troops. Along the way she met and married a Navy man, gained step-children, had a baby at 38, and lives and works happily from her home in Pensacola, Florida.

VirtualMVP
Pensacola, FL • 850-484-4184 • www.VirtualMVP.com

DJ Watson

Working in Your Bunny Slippers

The secrets of working from home and loving it!

Everyone wants to work from home. What's not to like – going to work in your bunny slippers, no dress code, making your own hours, flexibility, no more commuting, being able to be home with your kids, and low overhead.

As you can imagine, there is more to it than that – or else everyone would be doing it. I learned about working from home at an early age – my parents were both home-based entrepreneurs. My father, a farmer, never worked outside our home, save for a short two-year stint helping his cousin with a family business. My mother, a professional chef, ran a catering business from our home when I was in high school – guess where I worked on weekends.

So, it is probably no surprise, when after ten years in the corporate world, I started my own home-based business in 1994. I have been happily working in "my bunny slippers" since then. The following quote from my friend Martha, sums it up for me very nicely: "Recently I came across a folded sheet of paper tucked between two pages in one of my older journals. As I unfolded it, I could see that the words were faded and the date revealed it had been written about eight years ago. One of the goals stated that some day I would have "a corner office with a window." At the time I was working for a company that had an entire floor of cube stations. Mine was located midway to the center and just to the left of the corporate offices. Today, I have a home office located in the sunroom of my home. It is on the second floor and surrounded by trees allowing the sunlight to flicker through the branches and onto my desk. Behind my desk is a wall with one single window and a door that opens onto a small deck where I frequently enjoy an early morning cup of coffee as I collect my thoughts and plan my day. Little did I know at the time I wrote this goal that I would one day have my "corner office with the windows" and that it would be conveniently located in the comfort of my own home".   Martha Lanier, Professional Speaker, Author & Life Coach, Atlanta, GA.

I love Martha's story – and she would be the first to admit that getting there (and staying there) is not all wine and roses. It takes hard work and dedication as well as a little planning to be successful working from home. I have learned some things along the way, which is what I am sharing with you in this chapter. In addition to the pearls of wisdom I gleaned from watching my parents and from my own experiences, I polled colleagues and friends for their best tips on working from home, and I am including them here for you. Read on to find out if working from home is a realistic option for you and your career goals.

Whether you plan on starting your own business (self-employment and usually a sole-proprietorship) or telecommuting (working for a company or organization from your home), you will want to consider some factors about your personality, economics and preferences before you dive in.

GETTING STARTED

When I started my home-based business, I worked from a makeshift desk made up of a piece of wood and two filing cabinets. I was not too concerned about appearance, since clients of my Professional Organizing business were never going to see my office (although many wanted to). The desk had multiple advantages – it was inexpensive, sturdy, and efficient.

I was more concerned with the basics of a good home office set up, which included choosing supplies and equipment that would allow me to do what I needed in the most efficient manner. In order to decide what that means for your home office, ask yourself some questions:

- Do you use the office solely for business or also personal use?

- Are other people going to use the office?

- Are clients ever going to come to the office?

- Are you on the phone or the computer a lot?

- Will you store supplies, inventory and papers in the same space?

Location is another important factor in setting up a home office. For instance, if clients will come to your home, you may want to consider a space with a separate entrance, so clients do not have to come through private areas of your home. Whenever possible, make sure the office is its own space, not the dining room table. It can be a spare bedroom, a converted garage or, as in my current situation, a portion of the specially designed sunroom. I have even successfully operated my office from a corner of the den with a good partition. The trick here is to have a space that can be closed off.

You will need two items of furniture and they should be of excellent quality – a file cabinet and a desk chair. An ergonomically sound chair will make your life so much easier if you spend a lot of time at your desk and a good filing cabinet is worth its weight in gold. You can download a sample office supply list at www.VirtualMVP.com under the working from home section.

EQUIPMENT

Another area not to skimp on is the phone system. For anyone in business, a separate phone line is imperative. If you are still on a dial-up modem for your computer, consider a third line for computer and fax. You can use the house line for incoming calls, but it just does not sound professional when someone is yelling "Mom, pick up the phone!" You may want to consider a cell phone as your business line. Competitive rates and packages make this an attractive alternative to the expensive business lines that often cost double the rate of a residential line. (Note that giving up a business line may mean losing a space in the Yellow Pages.) Then you can add a second residential line for faxes, computer and outgoing calls if you wish. In any case, do add voicemail to your phone line so that if you are on the phone, you will not miss calls. Nobody wants to hear a busy signal.

Equally as important is to have high quality software. That means you should upgrade from the sample package that came with the computer if you are doing any significant work using the computer. At a minimum, a good business package has excellent word processing, accounting and database software. Most importantly – learn to use your software to its fullest capabilities. There are many inexpensive courses you can take online or in person.

GET ORGANIZED – THE BEAUTY OF GOOD SYSTEMS

Setting up a home office and starting a business involves a lot of trial and error. One thing that is not optional is to plan for growth. You start out operating from a shoebox, providing your services, happy to be in business. But, if you do not have some sort of system in place and keep good records, it becomes very difficult to grow your business. Adding staff or subcontractors, moving to a commercial location or even selling the business to another entrepreneur will be more difficult if you lack formal business systems. Having formal procedures makes your business more valuable. Consider starting your Office Procedure Manual from the first day on. Store these types of documents in one, easy-to-reach place. This includes a list of equipment, warranties and instructions, instructions on how you answer your phone, templates and forms used in your business, key personnel, client, and supplier information, and the location of important documents.

Think big, from day one. Assign jobs to yourself as if you were a major company. Create job descriptions. If you think about yourself as a company, eventually you will need to hire someone. When that happens, you will already have the tools in place.

A good filing system is a must. Even though 80% of what we file may never be looked at again, you need a "finding system" for you and for others to find things when your business grows beyond a sole-proprietorship. Take a look at the resource page on my website for excellent organizing tools to make this part easier.

Sue Estes, a Virtual Assistant in San Jose, CA, is a firm believer in the TO DO list. "The one thing that keeps me most focused and productive is writing a detailed TO DO list, so each night, I spend a few minutes jotting down tasks, errands, etc. which must be accomplished the next day". I too, could not live without my calendar and time planning system, and have learned through the years to jot down my 5 goals for the following day – that is my "A" list. If I get all 5 items accomplished, I move on to my "B" list – and I feel very productive when I get to cross 5 things off a 5-item list.

KIDS, SPOUSES AND OTHER PESTS

Time management is vital to the success of your new arrangement. Kathryn Willet, of Boynton Beach Florida, is a work-from-home mom. While operating an awards and incentive business, she has learned: "To really designate your time for work and not to waver from that. Tuesdays and Thursdays are my most productive days, and as the years have gone on I have made those days "work only" days. I do not do lunches (business or personal), run any errands, schedule any appointments, and my car pool partner even drives the kids to school. It makes the days that were always productive initially even more so. Mondays, when I am tired and grouchy anyway, I concentrate on errands and housekeeping chores like laundry. Wednesdays are a mix and Fridays, if I am caught up, can be a fun day or a work catch-up day, whichever I choose. I generally do work Saturdays, and enjoy it because my husband is in charge of the kids."

Make it clear to your family that you are working from home – and that your space and work hours must be respected. Even though you are working from home, it is essential to have some sort of child care arrangement for smaller children in order to be able to have some quality work time. When my son was very little, I had a nanny in my home – young college students who were glad for the job. Now, that he is in pre-school, I have a few hours a day to work uninterrupted.

Be sure to explain to neighbors and spouses that just because you are home, you cannot be expected to be there for pest-control appointments, parcel delivery, errand running or other conveniences during your work hours. You have a job just like everyone else – even if it is in your home. For more tips on coping with the work-from-home challenges, here is what Karen MacFarland Payne, a Professional Organizer in Waukesha, Wisconsin, had to say. "Have your in-office times as sacrosanct and rigid as possible. Resist putting a load of laundry in the dryer – the buzzer will go off, and there you are! Try not to mix domestic/business chores and hours (easier said than done, I know!)."

COPING AND SURVIVING

My friend and colleague, Anne Johnson, a software-coach and computer consultant in Pensacola, Florida, has this advice to share: "Working from home can be both exhilarating and isolating. One of the keys to staying sane and productive is to have a diverse group of colleagues and friends with whom you can carry on phone and/or email conversations. No matter how productive you are, you will have times where you need to hear a friendly human voice or just complain about your inability to connect with the decision-makers you are trying to reach. It is important that your circle of contacts include people who also work from home; however, it doesn't hurt to have some contacts who are working within the industry or corporate environment with which you perform your services or sell your product. This group of contacts can provide you with invaluable advice on the next step you need to take or simply provide support on a bad day. Creativity can stagnate, so the ability to send a quick email or phone request for information, feedback or commiseration is vital to your sanity! "

Finally, and most importantly, be prepared to leave the office at the end of the day and at the end of the week. It is tempting, when working from home, to go beyond regular office hours and spend free and family time "just catching up". In order to find balance and happiness in your life - and not to risk the wrath of those sharing your household – close the office door when work hours are over.

THE REST OF THE STORY

For more information on how this chapter continues to be updated on our website, please refer to the resource section at the end of this book. Online, you will find a continuation of topics discussed here, along with links to other resources and free articles and tip lists for download.

Working from home is not an easy task – bunny slippers or not. It is no easier than starting any business. It takes tenacity, a clear vision and passion. And it has been the best decision of my life. Step one for you is to take the assessment to see if working from home is for you. If you decide to forge ahead, drop me a line, I'd love to know how you are doing.

ARE YOU SUITED TO WORK FROM HOME?

Complete the assessment on the following two pages to determine if you are ready to embark on a home-based career.

Rate your answers on a scale of 1-5, with 5 representing the highest level of competency. Then note each score to the right of your response.

1=None 2=Somewhat 3=Practicing 4=Progressing 5=Accomplished

Motivation

Do you like responsibility? _____

Are you a self-starter? _____

Do you know what motivates you? _____

Do you need instant results to be motivated? _____

Organization

Are you easily distracted? _____

Are you a good time manager? _____

Can you handle multiple projects? _____

Can you follow through and finish a task even it if it is boring or distasteful? _____

Preferences

Do you like variety? _____

Do you want better work/life balance? _____

Do you need interaction with others? _____

Do you mind leaving corporate America? _____

Qualification

Are you interested in gaining new skills? _____

Are you a good project manager? _____

Are you a good problem solver? _____

Are you focused and not easily dissuaded? _____

Reality Check

Can you afford to work from home? _____

Do you have the right equipment? _____

Have you thought about child care? _____

Have you researched a viable work from home option? _____

COMPOSITE SCORES

Now compile the scores you rated for the individual components of the assessment. This will give you an indication of areas where you think you are strong in starting a home-based career.

Area	Score
Motivation	___
Organization	___
Preferences	___
Qualification	___
Reality Check	___
Total	___

Use this scale to interpret your total score to determine the overall readiness to work from home.

0 to 20	Not Ready
21 to 40	Somewhat Ready
41 to 60	Practicing
61 to 80	Progressing
81 to 100	Accomplishing

Now that you have taken the assessment, you have hopefully gained a snapshot of where you are in the process and whether or not working from home is for you. If you think you are on the right track – carry on! My friend Lisa Bentson, who is the president of Ali Lassen's Leads Club, summed it up best: "Love what you do and it doesn't matter where you work. "

CAREER COMPASS
for Women

Additional Resources From Our Team Of Co-Authors

The Indispensable Guidebook for Women in the Workplace!

COMPLIMENTARY ARTICLES THROUGH WWW.ALLISONSPEAKS.COM
A+A=S Formula for Success
Simple Signals that Sabotage Clear Communications
How to Be Assertive without Being Pushy
It's EASY to Say No
The Art of Assertive Communication
Say Yes to You

EDUCATIONAL MATERIALS
Mission Possible IV
Allison joins noted authors and speakers Jack Canfield, *Chicken Soup for the Soul*, and Brian Tracy, *The Psychology of Achievement*, in a collection of strategies on becoming more successful. This engaging, easy-to-read format includes ideas from artists to athletes to entrepreneurs. $15; available through www.AllisonSpeaks.com.

Millionaire in the Mirror audiocassette program
Taped in front of a live audience, this 60-minute program addresses daily habits for filling your personal performance bank account. Allison reveals how to achieve excellence over perfection, the importance of dreams and goals, and actions needed to translate dreams into reality. It's a fun, motivating way to begin or end your day. $9.95; available through www.AllisonSpeaks.com.

Real Women Have Chipped Nails online-coaching
A monthly subscription service designed to create a more balanced and fulfilling life. Each monthly issue coaches you through key areas such as getting over guilt, dealing with the downside of success, getting along while you get things done and building a mastermind network. Monthly and yearly options available through www.AllisonSpeaks.com.

KEYNOTES AND WORKSHOPS
Real Women Have Chipped Nails – life balance and self-management strategies
Flat Cats Don't Fly – make conflict comfortable and productive
Communicating with Tact and Finesse – what to say in difficult situations
SpeakEasy – persuasive and powerful presentation skills
How to Be Assertive without Being Pushy – get results with respect

GIFT IDEAS
Queen of the Universe T-shirt; $15
Tiaras; $4-10

800-664-7641or www.AllisonSpeaks.com

TRAINING TOPICS

A Place In Time offers a variety of training topics. All sessions are designed and adapted to individual needs. We work individually with each client to determine what the objectives and desired outcomes are.. The following list is designed to give you an idea of what topic areas are offered.

· Team Building
· Communications
· Problem Solving
· Customer Service
· The Fish Philosophy
· Who Moved My Cheese
· Creative Thinking
· Stress,Time & Conflict!!
· Developing Leadership Skills
· Effective Relationships
· Empowerment Strategies
· Humor in the Workplace
· Supervisory Techniques
· Behavioral Interviewing
· Performance Reviews
· Coaching for Success
· Process Improvement
· Discipline Issues
· & more..........

CONTACT INFORMATION

A Place In Time
Toni Boyles
PO Box 87
Tecumseh, KS 66542
785-379-8463
www.aplaceintimeonline.com

SEMINAR TOPICS

- Keys to Smart Hiring
- Fundamentals of Human Resources
- Recruiting and Retention
- Fundamentals of Help-wanted Advertising
- Elements of an Effective Ad
- Ad Construction

PROGRAMS

- Effective Supervision, a 2-1/2 day program for supervisors and managers.
- Strategic Recruitment, a customized approach to effective recruitment.

CONTACT INFO
To book Anne Craigs for a
speaking engagement or seminars,
call 866-657-5444 or
email info@employmenttimesonline.com

I Want to See the Jalapeno Coming (Creative marketing deck $10)
Follow the 28-step process and learn how to turn a creative concept into a
profitable plan. This product was developed to help people become more creative in their projects. Whether it is to improve your sales and marketing techniques or to plan a better social event, this system can work for you! The deck
contains 28 cards to lead you step-by-step through the process.

> "I was so enthused with your talk, I couldn't wait to get home and
> put the steps into motion selling our sassy new board game!"
> – Mary Merrell, Co-inventor of "Heels!" a board game for women.

20 Ideas that an Change Your Life (Compact Disc $17)
This dynamic program fits perfectly with the mission of helping people to
grow personally and professionally through leadership and education. Ideas
range from changes we can make in ourselves, with family, in the workplace,
and the community. This fast-paced program is guaranteed to make everyone
take time out to think. It's a great gift too!

> "It is always a pleasure to listen to you. You always offer a bigger
> outlook on life!" – Yvonne Dewey, Insurance Agent

Words at Work: Strategic Actions in the Workplace (Audio Cassette $14)
Successful people are accomplished communicators as well as versatile leaders.
They know the benefits of self-instruction and audio education. This "buffet of
information" contains practical ideas for improving your career. Topics
include: better communication in the workplace, advice for new managers,
attitude adjustments, become more productive, tough decisions made easier,
creative planning sessions, deal with interruptions, evaluation do's & don'ts,
four words as your motto and time management and much more.

> "The examples you gave us provided broad insights into how we can
> so things differently. Thanks for a first-rate program."
> – Marian Macief-Hiner, University of Wisconsin – Platteville

ORDERING INFORMATION:
Purchase on line at www.careercafe.biz
Or call toll free: 866-977-7325

Career Café
Box 724
DeKalb, IL 60115

AUDIO SERIES:

In Search of Normal: Moving Life From Chaos to Clarity
Are you in Search of Normal? According to the dictionary normal means: usual, typical, common, and routine. So if chaos is usual and dealing with stress is routine, then you are normal. If you don't like that definition, then what you want is a second definition, "to be free from emotional distress." If you want something different, you need to do things differently; that means, "Redefine your normal."
Learn how to:
• Put yourself first with the five Self-Health Habits
• Identify who's on your team and who's pretending to be
• Hold your Crazy Makers accountable
• Set boundaries and make *no mean NO*.
• Communicate your needs and wants
• Let others have your way
• Stop behavior that's sabotaging your own happiness and emotional well-being
• And much more!

BOOK:

I Want a Love Story to Happen to Me
Take a journey into the fairytale world of the Prince and the Princess and discover how they face the same real-life situations you do. This heartwarming poem will make you laugh, cry, and reflect on the fairytale side of your own relationship. This book makes a perfect gift.

MOST REQUESTED LIVE PROGRAMS:
• In Search of Normal: Life Balance & Stress Management
• Tapping into Your Team's Power Traits
• Communicating With Tact
• Dealing With Difficult People
• Powerful Presentation Skills

Be sure to check Cindy's website for new releases and to find out more about her "Edutaining" programs.

ORDERING INFORMATION
1-888-KUBICA4
615-726-4995
www.kubicaspeaks.com

Additional Resources From Ann Mah

Get reprints of Ann's articles from HersKansas magazine to grow your business skills. Articles include:

"Mentoring Teamwork" – Identifying a mentor can be the missing link when you're trying to make connections or find a friendly ear.

"Work Past 'No'" – Women don't have to be on the wrong side of the negotiating table. Play up your bartering strengths.

"30 Seconds" – Does your personal style open doors for your career, or is the door getting slammed in your face? Discover the secrets to making waves.

"Casual or Casualty?" Don't "dress down" your career aspirations by not looking the part.

"Let's Do Lunch" Follow the rules when dining out to get a step ahead in your career.

"Can You Hear Me Now?" Evaluate how you communicate to make sure you're getting your message across.

"Find the Leader in You" Think credibility, vision and communication when stretching your skills.

"Working From Home" Don't forget to find time for yourself when your office and home are the same place.

"Lower Your Center of Gravity" Seize control of your schedule to help maintain balance in your life.

"Go With the Flow" Change is inevitable at work, but you can make it easier on yourself.

"Stand Up and Be Heard" Giving a speech entails much more than the words you use.

"When Bad Behavior Happens to Good People" Strategies for dealing with conflict in the workplace.

Price: $2.00 each or the entire set of 12 for $15.00, including shipping.

ORDERING INFORMATION:
Phone: (785) 266-9434
Website: www.annmah.com
Email: ann@annmah.com

CD
"Turning Negativity into Possibilities"
Produced by Inspired Life Development, 2003
$21.00
Motivational CD program focuses on how to stay positive and keep the contagious effect of negativity from rubbing off on you. Also included are strategies for responding to communication challenges at work and at home.

BOOK
"The Productivity Path: Your Roadmap for Improving Employee Performance"
Maracom Publishing Company, 2001
$14.95
Sarita's chapter in this book focuses on how to give constructive criticism or confront negative situations without destroying employee performance.

ORDERING INFORMATION:
Sarita Maybin
Oceanside, CA
1-800-439-8248
(760) 439-8086
www.SaritaTalk.com

VIDEOS
Step Up and Lead 4 part video series

Step Up and Lead features Susan Meyer, award-winning international speaker and trainer. Our corporate training videos focus on leadership skills, leadership image, mastering motivation, mediation of employee conflicts, employee development and performance. Only $99.00 plus shipping and handling for all four videos. Set Includes:
Video 1: Establishing Yourself as a Leader (1hr 45min)
Video 2: Creating Synergy Through People Skills (1hr)
Video 3: The Leader as Coach: How to Bring out the Best in Individual Team Members (1hr 45min)
Video 4: Solving Performance Problems (45min)
Also available individually for $29.95 plus shipping and handling.

BOOKS
SOS! 101 Solutions to Overcome Stress, is our book filled with practical and humorous solutions for getting through stressful situations.
Available for $6.95 + S&H.
Speak with Power Passion and Pizzaz --333 tips to delight your audience. By Susan Meyer-Miller and Dr. Prasad Kodukula. 16.95 + S&H.

ORDERING INFORMATION:
SpeakerUSA
Susan Meyer-Miller
Shawnee, KS
1-877-674-8446
(913) 248-1485
www.SpeakerUSA.com

BOOKS BY HEIDI RICHARDS

Self Marketing Manual $67.00
A comprehensive marketing manual filled with "how to" ideas to market your business, create a publicity frenzy and become a "celebrity" in your community, your industry. Complete with dozens of forms (on disk) as well as the Self-Marketing Dictionary in PDF

Rose Marketing On A Daisy Budget $14.95
A simple down-to-earth book that shows you the "secrets" to marketing your small business on a tight budget.

Rose Marketing On A Daisy Budget Workbook $9.95
Workbook includes forms for "Assessing current business status," "Measuring customer service and satisfaction," "Developing direct mail promotions," and many more!

What's Your OccuPLAYtion? $7.95
149 Ideas to Increase Job Satisfaction, Reduce Stress, & Get More Out of Your Work & Your Life

"Yes" Is Only The Beginning $5.95
The Ideal Wedding Planner - Traditions, Etiquette & Checklists to Help you Plan the "Perfect Wedding."

E-BOOKS

Show Her the Money $11.97
The Women's ECommerce Handbook for Collecting Payments Online

Getting More Business $11.97
The Women's ECommerce Marketing Guide to Promote Your Products and Services on the Internet

Open For Business $11.97
The Women's ECommerce Guide to Starting a Successful Home-Based Business

Connected Through the Mouse $11.97
The Women's ECommerce Guide to Networking on the Web

ORDERING INFORMATION
Heidi Richards
800-466-3336
www.heidirichards.com

QUICK REFERENCE GUIDES

A Bitty Book of Basics series
• *Newsletters – Putting It All Together* $7.95
For the non-professional faced with preparing a company or organization newsletter. Covers basics steps for planning, designing, and distributing newsletters.

• *One Plus One Always Equals Two – Bookkeeping for Those Who Hate Math* $7.95 (available 12/03) For the non-accountant who needs to track business activity or just wants to better understand the information provided by the CPA. Includes terminology and basic benchmarks.

Briefcase Books series
• *SITS – Say It Through Symbols* $4.95
Fun booklet of acronyms and emoticons commonly used in e-mail messages.

SEMINARS AND WORKSHOPS

Computer and Computer Software instructional workshops
• Microsoft Office products
• Basic computer and Windows
• Internet – set-up, e-mail and searching
• Using scanners and digital camera
• QuickBooks and Quicken

Desktop publishing seminars
• How & Why – Making Your Newsletter Newsworthy
• Small Business Marketing thru Newsletters and Brochures

Bookkeeping seminars
• Payroll Management Stress – Identifying and managing forms and due date requirements

CONTACT:
Office Helpline
PO Box 442398
Lawrence, KS 66044
p) 785-843-8521
f) 785-843-0933
e) officehelpline@usa.net
w) www.officehelplineinc.com

OVER 60 TRAINING PROGRAMS

Creative Business Solutions can assist you with over 60 training programs on human resource issues, team issues, customer service, leadership and other topics.

In addition, we offer the following services:
• On-site Customized Training
• Management Assessment, Goal Setting and Coaching Support
• Team Consulting
• Human Resources' Assessment, Consulting and Support
• Process and Technology Consulting and Reengineering
• Multi-rater (360) Performance Assessment Systems

INSCAPE PUBLISHING ASSESSMENTS

We carry Inscape Publishing Assessments that you can use to help you move forward. Each of these will evaluate your skills in that area plus provide a tutorial to increase your skills.
These include:
• Coping with Stress Profile
• Leadership Profile
• Work Expectations Profile
• Personal Listening Profile
• Discovering Diversity Profile
• Time Mastery Profile

ORDERING INFORMATION

For more information, or to order one of the assessments, contact Creative Business Solutions at 785-233-7860 or 800-635-2310 or visit us at www.cbsks.com

LIVE PROGRAMS
Vicki Trembly is available for 1/2 day or full day workshops. Contact Vicki for rates and availability at 785-224-5408.

CRANIAL AEROBICS WORKOUT BAG
Includes a basic equipment for the exercises outlined in Vicki's chapter for Career Compass for Women, as well as instructions for additional exercises. Includes a brightly colored bag.

ORDERING INFORMATION
Send $25 check or money order
+$5 shipping and handling to:

Cranial Aerobics Workout Bag
Vicki Trembly
5440 SW 10th Street
Topeka, KS 66604
e-mail trainervik@cranialaerobics.com
www.cranialaerobics.com

30 Days to Getting Organized (booklet)
A day-by-day guide to 30 quick things you can do right now to clean up the biggest problems cluttering your life! This is not just a booklet - it is a program. Downloadable e-book - $ 6.00

TeleTips (booklet)
A 16-page booklet filled with over 70 time savers for phone, fax and e-mail. Includes the famous "eat a live toad first thing in the morning" tip, an e-mail glossary and much more. Downloadable e-book - $ 6.00

The Best ACT!™ Manual Ever!!
"Neglected customers never buy, they just fade away!" ACT!™ is a complete client relationship management system that allows you to track client contacts, phone calls, email and other correspondence with a click of your mouse. You can schedule and track activities with your contacts, as well as keep detailed notes and histories for each. This manual, will teach you to work with your contacts and data entry, categorize your contacts, create lookups, schedule events, organize your days, customize your screen layouts, customize your toolbars and menus, set   your preferences, correspond using ACT!™ and performing maintenance.
Additionally we offer a two-hour teleclass to coach you to achieve the above, email us for more information and receive a $15 credit if you order the teleclass within 60 days. $ 29.95 Downloadable E-book.

www.VirtualMVP.com – Free articles, tips and products for marketing and business support.

www.VitalAssitant.com – Find a Virtual Assistant to help you with all your projects.

www.sorganized.com – get organized!

ORDERING INFORMATION
DJ Watson
www.VirtualMVP.com – Your Marketing VP
A division of sorganized™

6550 Rambler Drive
Pensacola, FL 32505
850-484-4184/4111
Toll Free: 866-948-9020
djw@VirtualMVP.com